EARTH

The Conservation and Repair of Bowhill, Exeter: Working with Cob

(Frontispiece) Bowhill, South Range interior, section of cob wall prior to plastering. The area illustrated is between the posts of two jointed crucks, ie timber posts set in the wall and in this case jointed at their heads to the supporting roof-structure of the building. It shows original *c* 1500 plaster hacked (keyed) to take later seventeenth- or early nineteenth-century plaster (which has left a red/brown stain on the earlier work), in turn removed in 1978, with exposed *c* 1500 cob and *c* 1994 cob repairs. Note the *c* 1500 rubble packing against the right-hand jointed cruck post and *c* 1994 lime-mortar dubbing-out to the rubble packing of the left-hand post. Towards the wall-base are a number of *c* 1994 trial plaster patches. At the wall-head is *c* 1994 mortar 'make-up', continuously filling the original shrinkage gap between the cob and the underside of the eaves-purlin which spans between jointed cruck posts and which supports the rafter-ends.

ENGLISH HERITAGE

ENGLISH HERITAGE RESEARCH TRANSACTIONS

RESEARCH AND CASE STUDIES IN ARCHITECTURAL CONSERVATION

EARTH

The Conservation and Repair of Bowhill, Exeter: Working with Cob

Ray Harrison

Volume **3**

July 1999

JAMES X JAMES

First published by James & James (Science Publishers) Ltd, 35-37 William Road, London NW1 3ER, UK

A catalogue record for this book is available from the British Library
ISBN 1 873936 64 8
ISSN 1461 8613

Author: Ray Harrison
Series editor: Jeanne Marie Teutonico, English Heritage
Consultant editor: Kate Macdonald

Printed in the UK by Alden Group Ltd

Contents

Acknowledgements

The record of the building repair and reinstatement project was commissioned by Francis Kelly, English Heritage Inspector of Ancient Monuments & Historic Buildings, on behalf of English Heritage South West Region. The parallel and complementary work of Alfred Howard, master builder, and Larry Keefe, cob consultant, have been a constant inspiration. Larry has contributed part of the commentary on the soils used at Bowhill in Chapter 2.

At former London and regional management level, the author will always have a debt to repay to other former colleagues: to Beric Morley, Brian Field RIBA and John How RIBA for allowing him in on the job, to Richard Baker for his deep commitment to the works, to Arthur McCallum, English Heritage engineer for his belief in cob and daub and his inspired analysis of the jointed-cruck rearing and construction process; and to Tony Hansford and, latterly, Tony Leech, Technical Officer and Clerk of Works at Bowhill. Works contract photographer David Garner must be thanked for the excellent photography, managed with consummate thoughtfulness and tact; without it the story could not have been told.

The most important acknowledgement must be to those who brought about the practical realization of

English Heritage's plans for the building. These were the members of English Heritage's former Directly Employed Labour (DEL) teams in the south west working at the site between 1978 and 1995 (Fig 1). Those of the works staff with whom the author was most closely associated were: (based at Bowhill) Charles Smith, mason and site agent; Harold Partridge, carpenter chargehand; Andy Cribbet, mason; Paul Baker, carpenter; Mark Joy, labourer: (based at Berry Pomeroy Castle) Tony Stoyles, mason chargehand; Frank Lawrence, mason; Tom Perring, mason; Dave Heanon, labourer: (based at Okehampton Castle) Boysel Welham and Mike Perrett, masons: (based at English Heritage's former Totnes Workshops) Bernard Courtney, painter: and (based at Cleeve Abbey) Robin Court, mason chargehand. Other staff working for three months or more, at various times at Bowhill were John Lindon, site agent; Donald Coleman, superintendent; Bob Cox, carpenter; Jim Sullivan, carpenter; Martyn Clough, carpenter; Paul Blatchford, mason; and P. May and P. Maskell, carpenters/chargehands. Seconded from Okehampton Castle were Pat Hynes, mason/chargehand; Bob Kenchington, chargehand; Gerald Bird, mason (now Superintendent of Works); Ivan Bevan, labourer: from Berry Pomeroy Castle, Mary Jordan, mason: from Totnes Workshops, Tom Pace, carpenter/chargehand; Stuart Wilson, Gerald Widdicombe and John Roddy, carpenters: from Launceston Castle, Jim Dunn, mason: from Cleeve Abbey, Tony Bryant, labourer. Also associated with the works were R. Reed, E. Burnell, C. Parsons, M. Townes, P. Donmer, C. Proctor, L. Wills and R. Davies. Local and regional management involved were Tom Williams, area foreman; Roger Scobie, divisional DEL manager, former carpenter and chargehand at Bowhill; Tony Hansford, mason/superintendent; Donald Coleman, superintendent; Niall Morrissey, carpenter/superintendent; Tony Leech, mason/clerk of works and Doug Evans of DS Evans, Architects, who helped specify the repairs in the West Range; and Adam MacKenzie, stone mason, the last in a long line of Regional Superintendents of Works. A special debt is due to Charles Smith, Tom Williams, Harold Partridge, Mark Joy, Frank Lawrence, Tom Perring, Boysel Welham, Mike Perrett, Roger Scobie and Adam Mackenzie; without their help the making of this record would not have been possible.

Jeanne Marie Teutonico and John Fidler, of English Heritage Architectural Conservation Team, are also thanked for their efforts in bringing this book to a published state.

Figure 1 The Bowhill works team at the time of the completion of the new cob wall (seen behind them), 1992. Back row, (left to right) Ivan Bevan, Tom Williams, Tony Stoyles, Mark Joy, Jim Sullivan, Mike Perrett; front row, (left to right) Tom Perring, Boysel Welham, Frank Lawrence, Stuart Wilson, Harold Partridge.

Author

Ray Harrison has experience both as a local authority Conservation Officer and as a Historic Properties architect within English Heritage. Traditional earth building has been his special interest for twenty years. He is a founder member of the Devon Earth Building Association (DEBA) and a member of the ICOMOS UK Earth Structures Committee.

Preface

This technical record, which we hope will be useful in relation to clay-cob and its repair, arises from important work, begun under the Directorate of Ancient Monuments & Historic Buildings (DAMHB) and continued by English Heritage, at Bowhill, a Devon mansion of *c* 1500, now a part of Exeter. The house was taken into state ownership as a building at risk and has now been leased back to a local historical group, the Devonshire Association. Bowhill exhibits important architectural characteristics for which it is justly famous, most notably the remarkable roof structures associated with a late medieval carpenters' workshop centred at Exeter. Less well-known is the incorporation in this high-status building of a large amount of cob; in fact Bowhill is essentially a building of cob construction.

The restoration begun by DAMHB and the work of rebuilding and repair pioneered at Bowhill by English Heritage in the early 1990s were intended to be didactic: to raise levels of appreciation of this little understood and, even now, under-valued building technique which is so particular to Devon, but which is widespread in much of England and in the rest of the world (it is estimated that one-third of the world's population still lives in earth structures).

English Heritage is particularly keen to promote the repair of cob buildings and of earth structures generally in England. The repairs carried out at Bowhill are thus of great importance since they prove that it is possible to repair clay-cob successfully. The work was essentially non-structural. Other opportunities for serious structural repairs have subsequently arisen in the region, notably at Bury Barton, Devon, and Cullacott, Cornwall, where English Heritage grant-aided work undertaken by private contractors to restore important cob buildings. As a result of the pioneering work at these three Devon sites, the technical issues surrounding cob can now be addressed from a position of greater understanding. In particular it is recognised that successful cob repairs can only be executed if there is an understanding of the techniques involved by both specifier and craftsman and that they cannot be executed without detailed specifications. The wider publication of the work at the three sites should be an invaluable aid to this. Detailed technical reports (1995, 1996) on both the other projects were commissioned from Larry Keefe by English Heritage.

The spin-offs have been valuable and parallel developments encouraging; first the emergence of the Devon Earth Building Association (DEBA), now federated under the ICOMOS UK Earth Structures Sub-Committee, then of earth-construction modules and research at Plymouth University. This study has an important place in the gathering momentum of understanding cob, especially of its repair, in Devon.

The study also includes a short section on single-coat lime plasters. The slate roofing at Bowhill has prompted an academic article about traditional slating in Devon in *ASCHB Transactions* 12 (1990), and a technical evaluation (forthcoming). The changing approaches to conservation exhibited at Bowhill are the subject of a further article by Ray Harrison in *ASCHB Transactions,* 20 (1996); finally an academic monograph on the structural development of Bowhill is planned (Blaylock, forthcoming). Something for every taste!

Dr Kevin Brown
Director
English Heritage South West
April 1999

Foreword

This study presents some of the detail of a series of repair and reconstruction works, the majority of which were undertaken between 1990 and 1995 as part of the rehabilitation of Bowhill. The works of particular concern here involved cob and daub – unbaked earth construction. These are indigenous West Country materials and techniques, largely fallen out of use, but experiencing a not inconsiderable revival in the region today. In fact the 'rediscovery' of cob is part of a wider reawakening of interest in the material and the buildings, not only in Britain but also immediately across the Channel in northern France and further afield.

The first part of the study, Chapter 1, puts the building and the works into a broad context, and gives some background by explaining the role of the state in the direct conservation of historic buildings, describing briefly the way in which this worked with individual sites. There follows Chapter 2, a limited examination of the former place of earth in building in Britain and, more specifically, the place of the Bowhill works within West Country tradition. The discussion in this chapter on the problem of building with earth is developed out of that in an earlier paper published in *Transactions of the Ancient Monuments Society* ns28 (see Bibliography – J R Harrison 1984). The final and main section, Chapters 3,4,5 and 6, presents summaries of a series of cob, daub and lime-based repair and rebuilding projects, and of controlled experiments in lime-based rendering, all carried out at Bowhill from 1990 to 1995. A glossary offering definitions of some of the more particular or arcane building and material terms used is also included.

While the bulk of the illustrations concentrate on repair, the central colour section tells a slightly different story. Here are highlighted the architectural qualities of space, detail and finish shown in the reinstated interior, the investigation and display of archaeological evidence, the visual and textural qualitites of the local red sub-soil in old and new walling, some aspects of original or secondary construction and working contexts where colour printing brings out the variety of materials that make the building.

English Heritage has leased Bowhill on a 125 year lease to the Devonshire Association for the Advancement of Science, Literature and the Arts. Visitors are welcome. Bowhill is open to the public from Easter to October by prior arrangement with the Administrator (01392 252461). Future plans include increased opening hours.

Ray Harrison

Key to the drawing convention

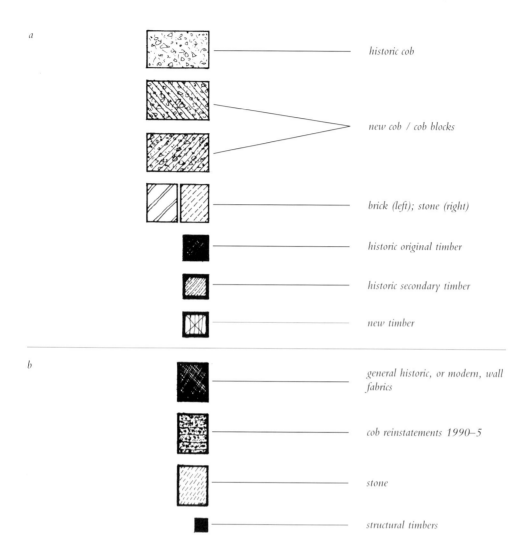

a

historic cob

new cob / cob blocks

brick (left); stone (right)

historic original timber

historic secondary timber

new timber

b

general historic, or modern, wall
fabrics

cob reinstatements 1990–5

stone

structural timbers

a   larger-scale drawings, orthagonal plans and sections only
b   intermediate scale sections and elevation drawings

In one or two cases where conventions are altered for clarity this
is noted on the drawing.

1 Introduction

The working-foreman in charge and the men he controls must have been trained in the tradition of sane repair under leadership such as is provided by the Society for the Protection of Ancient Buildings, or by the Ancient Monuments Department of His Majesty's Office of Works (Powys 1929 [1995], 5).

THE BUILDING

Bowhill is in the manor of Barley in St Thomas's parish, over a mile west of Exeter. It is on the Exeter to Moretonhampstead road, the direct but hazardous western route out of Exeter to Cornwall via the heights of Dartmoor, and looks back from the east-facing slope known as Dunsford Hill towards the towers of the Cathedral across the river Exe (Fig 2). Today the immediate view is over the roofs of suburban Exeter as the site is almost at the limits of the modern town; once it would have been over open fields and the original suburb of St Thomas's.

The building, which dates to around 1500, is best described as a small manor house or mansion.[1] It is typical of late medieval 'gentry' houses in its concern to display status, symbolized by the refinements of a double court-yard plan and an open hall, with, inside, enclosed hearths and chimneys and traditional features such as a screens passage and separate kitchen block. There is evidence for another, and quite different, house on the site before Bowhill was built. An excavated section of the base of this earlier building confirmed it as mud-walled, its walling built directly off the ground. Such construction was once common but mud walls of this type are of their nature less long-lived than those built off stone bases and are very rare in Britain today (they are still occasionally found in Devon, pers comm John Thorp).

Much of the layout of the house survives (Fig 3a). The two-storey open hall where the owners could hold court is in the east range at right angles to the road, sited to the rear, not unlike an urban medieval arrangement (Fig 4). The projecting east entrance porch, now lost, was itself a status symbol. A small service room to the north of the hall seems to have also had an upper storey with an external stair. The screens passage at the southern end of the hall linked to the kitchen in the west range by means of an external footway under a lean-to roof, a 'pentice', within the courtyard against the north side of the south range (Fig 5). Similar arrangements are to be seen elsewhere in the West Country.[2] The 'parlour', with a contemporary fireplace and moulded cross-beam ceiling, effectively the owner's private living room and perhaps office, abuts the south side of the screens-passage. Other rooms within the ground floor of the South Range may have had secondary functions such as storage (Fig 3a).

Above the parlour, and also possessing a fireplace and decorative ceiling, is the Great Chamber, another private apartment probably reached from a now lost block attached to the south east corner of the house. Scars on the surviving fabric show where this extension abutted the corner. The remaining two rooms within the first floor of the south range are known as the Inner and the Oriel chambers. The latter once had a projecting bay window, an oriel, and may have been a separate apartment. It may have had a steep ladder stair to the ground floor but seems also to have been reached by a stair and

Figure 2 Bowhill's east elevation during repairs, 1993. This shows the new cob to upper part of lean-to (right); stonework/windows with cob above (centre); stonework with lime-rendered timber panel to gable above (left).

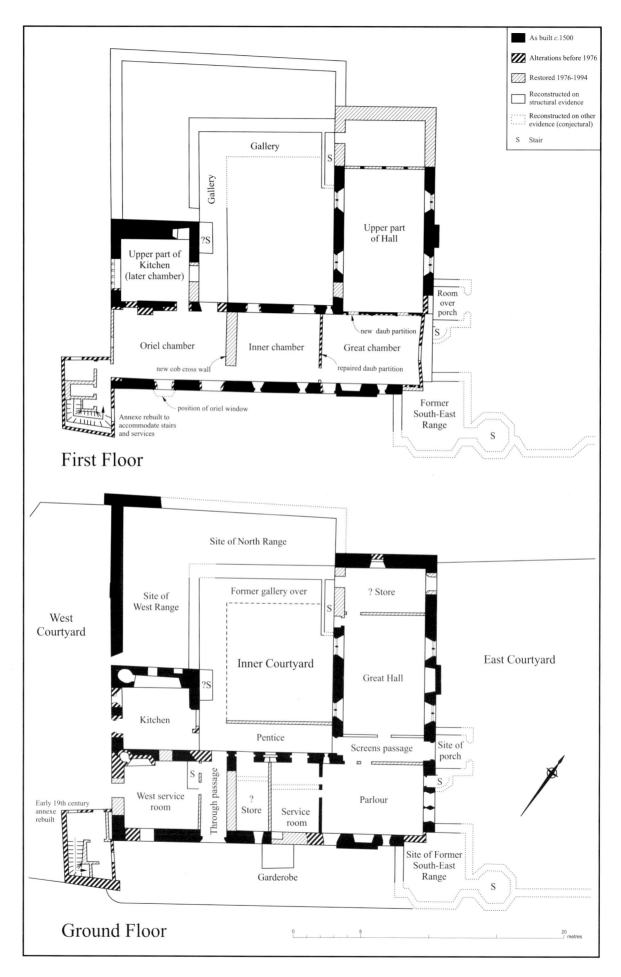

Figure 3 a (above) & b (top, facing page) Building plans and site plan. (Drawn by Exeter Archaeology)

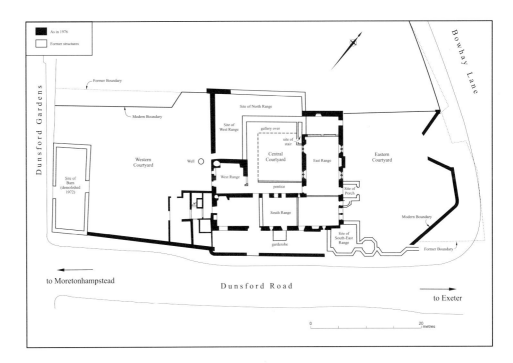

Fig 3 b

Figure 5 *View of the courtyard from the north west, 1995. Repairs are largely complete with the new pentice (lean-to passage-way) in place between hall (left); and kitchen (right). The lines of the courtyard wall-footings of the lost North and West Ranges are laid out in the foreground.*

Figure 4 *Great Hall after completion of repairs, 1993. The view is south, towards the screens passage and junction with the two-storey South Range.*

Figure 6 *The South and East Ranges in the 1960s. A large doorway towards the end of the south range gives access to the courtyard and the service-rooms to its south and west. (Copyright: Royal Commission on the Historical Monuments of England)*

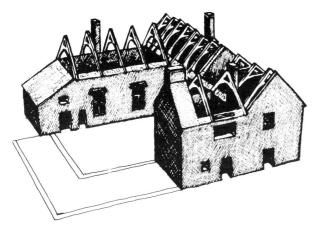

Figure 7 Bowhill: main structure, walls and roofs. All the main elements shown here survived in whole or in part, except for the lean-to at the north end of the Great Hall, which was in large part rebuilt, and the west gable. (Purlins and rafters omitted for clarity)

gallery within the courtyard. This latter stair is likely to have also given access to first floor rooms in the West Range which disappeared when the north end of this part of the building was demolished *c* 1800 (see Fig 3). There is evidence for this loss in a spread of cob found between two levels of 'metalling' in the courtyard. The surviving section of the West Range is occupied by the kitchen which, like the hall, was open to the rafters though, again like the hall, a first floor was inserted at a later date. Above ground nothing is left of the building that once closed the north side of the courtyard and its former use is uncertain. There was a second, more agricultural, courtyard up the hill to the west, from which a substantial barn remained until 1972 (see Fig 3b).

Bowhill is important among houses of its type and status in Devon because of the amount of original fabric that survives (Fig 7). Many other parallel cases in the county have suffered more alteration from later extensions and rebuildings. It is outstanding, even at the national level, because of the timber roof structures of the hall and great chamber. These, though they derive from the 'jointed-cruck' system of the western counties, have a number of special features including a continuous coving above the collar, curved feet to the wind-braces, distinctive intermediate trusses and moulded wall-head purlins (Fig 8). This type of roof, which is more for show than for strength, relates to a small but important group of local buildings which includes the Exeter Guildhall, the Deanery and Law Library in Exeter and Cadhay near Ottery St Mary. The design of these roofs represents a fusion of local and national carpentry traditions of the time, the work of a sophisticated regional school with a keen awareness of wider practice. Although somewhat reduced from its original size, the importance of Bowhill has been recognized since the mid nineteenth century on account of its open hall and for its distinctive roof structure.

EARTH FOR BUILDING AT BOWHILL

Large sections of the walls of Bowhill are built of 'cob' (Fig 12) while much of the interior wall panelling is in

Figure 8 Great Hall roof 1995, photo looking north, drawing looking south, showing principal characteristics: main and intermediate trusses; intermediate trusses appearing to 'ooze' around the heavy collar-level plates; continuous coving at the apex (formed with braces pegged by free tenons to the underside of the rafters); outward-curving feet to the lower end of the windbraces, where they double as ashlar-pieces. (Drawing by Piran Bishop of Exeter Archaeology)

'daub' (Fig 9). Both are derived from natural, unprocessed, earth. Before the industrial revolution this most flexible of materials was very widely used in construction of all sorts, being by no means always perceived as second rate. Indeed, Bowhill gives the lie to such assumptions; here is

Figure 9 Daubing in progress at the Great Chamber, Bowhill, 1990; Harold Partridge throwing daub.

a high-status mansion largely built in what is now regarded, with thatch, as the epitome of vernacular building materials in Devon. Today, however, an understanding of the potential of cob and of the skills and knowledge needed for its practical employment have been all but lost in this country, though earth continues to be an important vernacular material the world over.

Recent years have seen a gradually growing resurgence of interest in the preservation of the traditional earth buildings of Britain, a subject where conservation and green issues go hand in hand. A number of new earth structures have been built since the early 1980s and the study of appropriate repair is beginning to develop. The repair and reconstruction work called for at Bowhill offered an opportunity to contribute to this debate through the detailed examination of existing earth walling and through controlled experiment with the use of earth for repair and building work.

MANAGEMENT OF THE WORKS OF CONSOLIDATION AND REPAIR

Bowhill, which is now listed Grade I,[3] was taken into guardianship[4] by the state as a threatened building in 1976 (Fig 10). In 1984, English Heritage (the Historic Buildings and Monuments Commission for England)

took over responsibility for its repair and reconstruction from its predecessor the Directorate of Ancient Monuments and Historic Buildings at the Department of the Environment.

Buildings and sites in guardianship and in the state's ownership must be maintained and repaired, and until not long ago it was possible to find monument site works management procedures essentially unchanged for 70 or 80 years. Thus in 1981 it could still be said that,

> Since the first legislation ... the care of ancient remains has been regarded by the Government as a works function, settled on the Office of Works and its descendants ... day-to-day management of the monuments is in the hands of Architects, advised by Inspectors of Ancient Monuments (Thompson 1981, 11). [5]

The Architect/Inspector working relationship described here held good into the early 1990s in that part of English Heritage to which management of properties in guardianship had descended from the old Office of Works. It was thus in place for a large part of the duration of the Bowhill works. Also common until recently was the

Figure 10 The condition of the north internal gable wall of the Great Hall at the time the building was taken into state care. During conservation the modern tie beams were removed, as were the modern gable windows. The timber framing and infill were repaired and the ground floor brick panel was removed and replaced by timber panelling reconstructing the original arrangements. (Copyright: Royal Commission on the Historical Monuments of England)

out-stationing of permanently employed works staff, the members of English Heritage's former Directly Employed Labour organisation, the DEL[6]. These craftsmen, masons, carpenters, labourers, were dispersed in small groups at different monument sites up and down the country and could be brought together for major operations. These were the labour supply circumstances holding during most of the period of reconstruction and repair at Bowhill.

From 1993 to completion in 1995 'contractualization' replaced the last vestiges of the old DEL arrangements in favour of formal contractual relationships. Subsequently the DEL have been fully privatized under the name Historic Properties Restoration Ltd.

It varies from black earth to white chalk, from yellow clay through sandy clay to stoney clay and shillet, and some of these can be likened to mild concrete and are used as such to top-off masonry walls, form a bed for wall plates and to hold the pegs of the thatcher and the slate battens on the gables. Good cob can be moistened and re-used quite easily, but needs to be tamped down and compacted in the same way as concrete and mortar and plaster. [7]

Old cob never dies

(pers comm Alfred Howard, 1990).

EARTH AND THE BRITISH VERNACULAR WALL-BUILDING TRADITION

Before looking at the use of earth in the building and at the detailed management of the repairs, it will be useful to touch on the wider historic context and to consider the fundamental problems of working with cob and daub.

Earth used in building is invariably natural soil taken from below the humus-bearing ground level but above zones of very heavy clay or fractured bedrock. In Devon it takes the form of a mixture of clay (mineral) and some or all of silt, sand, gravel and even stone (Fig 11). Such natural deposits were dug up and mixed together with fibre and water, built while moist into walling and allowed to dry and set solid (Fig 12).

In Britain earth prepared in this way was used, among other things, as mortar bedding and wall-core 'hearting' in stone walls. Its main employment in quantity as a walling material, however, was either as daub or as solid 'mud' (cob) walling.

Solid earthen walling is similar in thickness to stone walling and was used in a similar way. The prepared raw material was known as mud in much of England, as 'clay' in the north, Scotland and Ireland, 'clom' in South Wales and of course 'cob' in the south west. It was piled up damp, in superimposed courses, to form the wall (see Harrison 1984).

The method was not susceptible to the variations possible with daub, some of which are discussed below. Differences in basic ingredients aside, a mud boundary wall varies little in whatever part of the world it is built. When it comes to the systems of construction within which mud plays a part, however, differences can be considerable, especially in matters of structural flooring and roofing. At root vernacular building methods in Devon and numbers of other highland [8] parts of Britain combined the mass mud or stone wall with a type of structurally semi-independent timber frame to accommodate the northern European rain-shedding steeply pitched roof. The key structural element here was the cruck, a timber A-frame combined in Devon with posts

Figure 11 Raw subsoil from excavation for a reservoir nearby, awaiting use at Bowhill, 1991.

Figure 12 500-year old cob in the top of the kitchen walls, slightly degraded, 1993.

Figure 13 A jointed-cruck principal in the Oriel Chamber, 1993. The roof load is carried down to floor level via posts recessed into the cob wall (left). The cob cross-wall closing the view is the reinstatement of the early 1990s, described later.

in the wall,[9] taking the roof load directly via the ridge, purlins and eaves purlins (Fig 13).

The recent history of Scottish pre-improvement building shows that mud might merely be one among a range of walling materials pressed into service as screening between the posts of load-bearing crucks. Other such materials have been wattle and daub, dry-stone, solid peat, peat block, turf block, layered stone and turf and turf tiles hung on wattling (see Fenton & Walker 1981). The particular significance of the Devon practice, however, is its demonstration of the clear longevity of the concept of the integration of the load-bearing cruck and the mass wall, the latter offering rigidity to the posts of the trusses but capable also in its own right of bearing load.

Daub, as in the term wattle-and-daub, is still familiar to people, even today. Earthen daub, as with cob a damp mix of earth and fibre, is plastered onto or into a timber framework to give a solid infill panel. There are innumerable international variations on the theme and, not surprisingly, in Britain the variety of systems developed in recent historical times was considerable.[10]

Timber reinforcing ties have been found within mud walls, and, it is said, sometimes even pegs between courses, and some daub walls are really more mud than daub. Documentary confirmation of the former overlap of plastering, daub and mud-walling comes in the medieval *Statute of Labourers* (1351) which puts the trades under the same head:

> plasterers and other workers of mud walls, and their mates likewise [shall have 3d and 1½d] from Easter to Michaelmas (Salzman 1952, 72).

That plasterers dealt as a matter of course with daub 'beam-filling'[37] as well as with lime and lime plaster is confirmed by a further record.

> ... at Brigstock Park a mason was employed, in 1423, to do what is called earth work (opus terr') defined as 'bemfyllynge werlynge (= wattling) pergetyng plastryring and wasshyng (elsewhere, whytlymyng)'. (Salzman 1952, 192).

In the West Country vertical panel support for daub, typical of eastern Britain, is not known, horizontal arrangements being preferred. A method that might be described as 'ladder rung' is common; earliest surviving examples date to the seventeenth century. Holes are drilled in the sides of fairly closely set vertical studs to accept the ends of horizontal staves one above the other like the rungs of a ladder. These support the daub which is applied from both sides. In Devon this type of panel is usually found inside buildings though cases of external use are known. Staves may be fixed at closer or wider centres. In Somerset in the early nineteenth century the method was recommended, along with mud, as producing 'the cheapest habitation that we can construct'.[11]

Figure 14 Ground-floor partition, south end of Great Hall after repair and reconstruction but before daub-infilling, 1987. Note the short stub-end reinforcing timbers. (Photograph: Exeter Archaeology)

Figure 15 Lathed daub panel between the Great Chamber and Inner Chamber, 1992. The lower section is lathed for the application of daub plaster, the upper for lime plaster. The lower laths are replacements for seventeenth-century originals.

At Bowhill a variant of ladder-rung in the form of studs carrying only the stub ends of the 'rungs' was found and repaired (Fig 14). It is a particularly ingenious combination of earth and frame.

If the horizontals of the ladder-rung are removed to the outside of the studs, or ceiling joists or rafters, and become nailed laths as in the backing for conventional lime plaster, daub can be applied on the same principle as plaster. This way of making ceilings was found at Bowhill. Richard Neve, writing on plastering in the early eighteenth century, notes:

> Experienced Workmen tell me, that it ought to be done upon Heart-laths ... And tho' it be more work to Lath it with Heart, than with Sap-Laths; yet 'tis better for the Mortar to hang to, because Hearth-laths are narrowest, and they ought to be closer together for Mortar than for Lome [sic] (Neve 1726, 99).

In this context 'lome' (loam) is another term for daub. In practice Neve's advice on lath spacing is found to be true for lime plasters, their heavier, homogenous mix hanging better on narrower-spaced lathing (Fig 15).

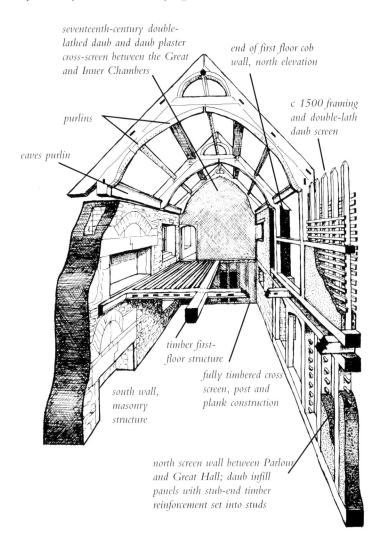

seventeenth-century double-lathed daub and daub plaster cross-screen between the Great and Inner Chambers

purlins

eaves purlin

end of first floor cob wall, north elevation

c 1500 framing and double-lath daub screen

timber first-floor structure

fully timbered cross screen, post and plank construction

south wall, masonry structure

north screen wall between Parlour and Great Hall; daub infill panels with stub-end timber reinforcement set into studs

Figure 16 (above) Bowhill, South Range: section looking west through structure of cob, daub partitions, masonry and floors, at Parlour (ground) and Great Chamber (first floor). The depth of the view is 'stretched' in order to show the various elements clearly (based on drawings by Exeter Archaeology). The photograph (above right) shows new daub packed behind, extruded through and beaten back onto new oak lathing, 1990.

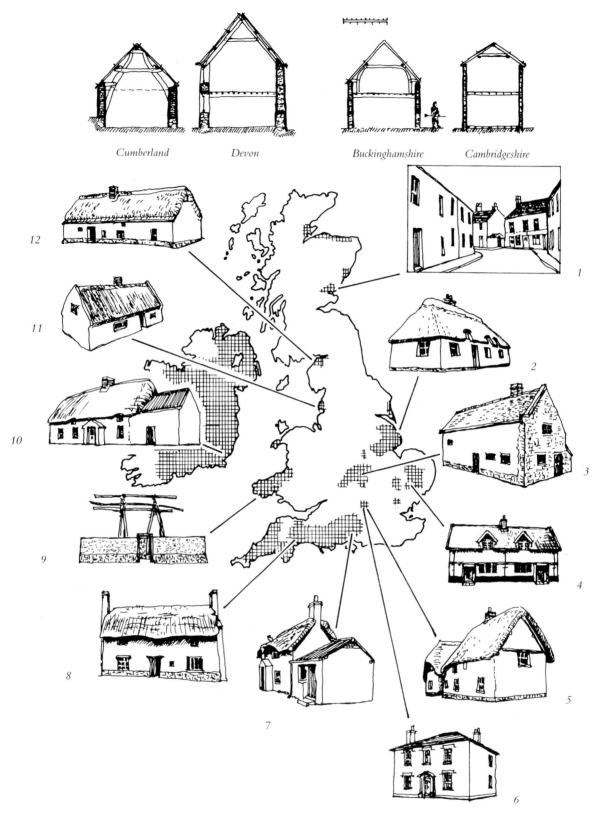

Cumberland   Devon   Buckinghamshire   Cambridgeshire

Figure 17 Cob buildings' distribution map, British Isles and Eire (copyright Ray Harrison, with acknowledgement to D Bouwens). The various illustrations of local vernacular traditions shown here are numbered clockwise, starting in eastern Scotland. (1) Perthshire (after Walker), Scots 'clay' terraces; (2) Lincolnshire 'mud' house; (3) Northamptonshire 'mud' and stone house; (4) Norfolk (East Anglian) 'improvers' 'clay lump' council houses; (5) Buckinghamshire 'wichert' farm houses; (6) Buckinghamshire 'wichert' polite house (an early nineteenth-century form also seen in other parts of the south); (7) New Forest 'mud' squatter house and stable; (8) Devonshire 'cob' farm house; (9) South Wales cottage, re-erection of 'clom' walls and cruck frame, St Fagans Folk Museum; (10) Irish 'mud' farm house; (11) Lancashire Fylde 'clat and clay' farm house (after Watson); (12) Cumbrian, Solway Plain 'clay' farm house and attached byre. The sections at the head of the page are taken from Harrison 1984. The map shows the spread, and a little of the variety of built forms, of the earth-building tradition as it survives today. It does not differentiate between areas where major concentrations of, or only a few, buildings survive. Key concentrations of mud buildings are in the south west of England. Almost everywhere else they are under serious threat of disappearance. (Illustrations and advice from M Andrew, P Barker, D Bouwens, J James, B Walker, R Watson and E Wiliam)

If we take things a stage further and attach the horizontal lathing to both sides of the vertical studwork, a daub-cored, double-lathed panel can be formed. This is a distinctly different arrangement from the hollow, framed wall, lath-and-plastered both sides. The daub filling as found in Devon is usually not less than 3–4" (75–100mm) thick, the stud thickness, and begins to take on a structural dimension by helping to keep the panel frame rigid (Fig 16). The system is found at Bowhill in both fifteenth- and seventeenth-century versions.[12]

The basic method is known the world over. It is a common feature of many traditional buildings in Africa, with core fillings of daub, bits of stone, broken brick or even vegetable matter. It is hardly known in Britain today outside the West Country. For other examples see Guerney Manor, Cannington, Somerset; Leigh Barton, Churchstow, Devon and the Totnes Museum, Fore Street, Totnes, Devon.

RECENT USE OF EARTH IN BUILDING IN DEVON

Mention has been made of the recent growth of concern over the conservation and preservation of historic mud buildings in Britain for which a distribution map is given (Fig 17).

Study of the practice is prefaced here by a review of previous and some related contemporary, developments in the modern use of earth in building in the West Country. The method there had long ago been in its death throes, even as the architect Clough Williams Ellis took his classic record at the end of the First World War (Williams-Ellis 1919 [1947]). Elsewhere in Britain it had been in general decline long before this. Rural tradition is tenacious, however, especially in the highland areas of the country. Devon tradesmen able to manage the material still existed after the last war, as they still do today, but lack of public support and interest was generally against them. Where the continuing use of cob remained appropriate, as with the reinstatement of perished beam-filling [37] at wall-tops during thatching, there it still found favour. Thatchers and farmers continued to prepare, remix and place small amounts of cob in such situations. The author has heard of bare-foot mixing in this context as well as of one Devon thatcher, who as late as 1980 was said to still flash the sides of chimney stacks with 'clay' (pers comm Charles Hulland).

In the late 1960s Clough Williams Ellis's work was again taken up when John Deal ARIBA ran a series of enthusiastic student working parties which carried out cob repairs to a farmhouse and steading at Dunsford, a task that extended over a number of summer seasons (Fig 18). The record of this work has unfortunately never been published and was followed by a long period of inactivity in the region.

Then in the early 1980s, Alfred Howard, a third-generation master builder from near Crediton, at that time in his mid 60s, turned his mind to passing on to succeeding generations of local builders what he had been taught of cob building by his father. In 1980, 'to

show them how to do it', he directed the building of what was probably the first serious new cob structure in Devon since the last war, albeit a mere bus shelter, but with a fine oak-framed and clay-pantiled roof; a gift to the parish of Down St Mary. He has continued the work into his 70s (Fig 19), going from strength to strength, a constant inspiration to those coming after him. [13] Of these latter must be mentioned Richard Tapp, builder, Alfred Howard's younger colleague; John Vicary and the architects, Paul Bedford (then of the Architecton practice) and Jonathon Rhind, whose separate structural repair works of the early 1990s are of much imaginative interest, and Larry Keefe, former Conservation Officer at Teignbridge District Council. The latter has pioneered research into the nature and performance of local Devon soils, work carried forward by him in his research at Plymouth University. He also managed the erection of Devon's first contracted cob building since the Second World War, a small park shelter at Starcross, near Dawlish, funded by Teignbridge District Council. More recently Larry Keefe has overseen major works of structural repair and reconstruction in cob at Bury Barton, an historic site in mid-Devon (Fig 20) and at Cullacott in North Cornwall.

As noted earlier, one of English Heritage's potential contributions to the debate in the South-West was through opportunities offered by the exemplary repair of their historic properties in the area. Experiments with reconstructed daub panelling began during works at

Figure 18 Jonathan Deal hands material up to the worker on the wall during cob repairs at Dunsford, Devon in the 1970s. Note plumber's lead-beater held by the worker for beating down new material on the wall. (Reproduced by permission of John Deal ARIBA, photographer Alastair Hunt.)

Figure 19 Alfred Howard outside his house at Down St Mary, Devon, 1994. To the right, the original historic cottage, to the left Mr Howard's new two-storey thatched cob extension with remarkable curved corner windows with oak lintels.

Leigh Barton near Kingsbridge in 1974. These trials under the Ancient Monuments architect, Harry Gordon Slade, only partially recorded, relied on stabilizing the daub by the addition of lime. They were followed by the first, and then second, stage trials at Bowhill; the latter discussed below, the former again under Harry Gordon Slade. The second stage trials coincided with the setting up of the Devon Earth Building Association by a group of individuals from various backgrounds dedicated to raising the profile of earth as a material for repair and building in the region. English Heritage's regional South

Figure 20 Barn porch of cob at Bury Barton, Devon, Grade II* farmyard, 1994. This shows major new cob reconstruction of pier, front and side elevation. Structural works designed and supervised by Larry Keefe and grant-aided by English Heritage, 1994.

West team was represented on the Association's working group and the organisation's contribution here was partly through the works at Bowhill. A number of open days and lectures at the site publicized the use of earth for repair. Interested private individuals were given the opportunity to gain experience by taking part in the work and the building site was always available by arrangement for guided inspection tours. In this way English Heritage's operations in repairing the building helped to underpin a significant local development in conservation awareness.

The total range of the earth repair and reconstruction managed at Bowhill is probably wider than that undertaken in any other standing building in Devon to date. Repair was, apart from a new cob cross-wall in the south range, largely restricted to non-structural aspects, since existing walls were generally structurally sound. Since then, the interest in and revival of building in cob in Devon has gathered momentum, as has, gratifyingly, the interest in and experience of repairing cob and daub. [14]

THE EARTH BUILDING AND OTHER WORKS AT BOWHILL

It is necessary to divide the trial works into two stages. Because there was little recording during the first stage full details are not presented here. Within the first stage, from 1978 to 1987, matters covered were the complete reinstatement of two kinds of daubed panel, the reinstatement of new cob walling, using earth/lime mixes, the laying of a new cob/lime floor and the application of interior lime plaster to the composite cob and stone walls of the hall. There were thus four main categories of semi-experimental project, ie new daub, new cob, new cob flooring and new plaster.

The second stage works were from 1987 to 1995; those reviewed here involved the works from 1990 onwards and covered the manufacture of the material, new cob-wall building and a variety of cob-wall repairs as well as wall building and repair in cob-block. Daub repair, new daub panelling (walls and ceiling) and daub plasters were examined along with limewash and plaster to daub and finally lime plaster and render to cob and stone. The main (experimental) categories reviewed here therefore are material preparation, new and repaired daub and cob, new and repair work in cob-block and new renders.

In cases where the reconstruction of missing elements is involved, an explanation for the form of reconstruction is given. The practical and philosophical justifications for reconstructions and for repairs generally are considered elsewhere in a separate paper (Harrison 1996).

Solutions to problems and approaches to managing earth at Bowhill are sometimes contrasted with those developed on other sites in Devon during the same period as well as with the historic record. Where possible performance in the completed work is commented on.

Because of English Heritage's system of commissioning and managing the works, discussed earlier, throughout the job there was much movement of labour between Bowhill and other local monument sites. At one point the site could be somewhat starved of workers while at another large numbers of staff might be available. When working with new cob this was often an advantage, since continuous building in cob is generally considered to be tricky. Even as far away as Cumberland it is possible still to be told that 'they liked to have more than one job on the go at once so as to let each new course go off properly before starting the next' (pers comm Brian Sinclair). At Bowhill these arrangements meant that time spent away from the site might sometimes be more than was needed to arrive at the point where work could be taken up again. Thus the start-to-finish timescale of the cob and daub works is not necessarily a reliable reflection of the time actually needed to complete things. Details of the time these tasks took are not, therefore, generally included in the works review.

A further aberration in the way matters at Bowhill were managed relates to the round-the-year working practiced at the site. Some of the earth works were done over the winter, under cover, with no deleterious effect, other than painfully slow drying-out. Traditional wisdom, in the form of Alfred Howard, advises for obvious reasons that 'building should start when the birds begin to build their nests and the roof should be on when they begin to lose their feathers'. Startlingly similar advice is given in Loudon (1836) where it is said that 'in Devonshire, the builders of cob-wall houses like to begin their work when the birds begin to build their nests, in order that there may be time to cover in the shell of the building before winter' (Loudon 1836, 417).

Finally, the extent of the record of the controlled experiments at Bowhill must be defined. From 1990, planning for the trials as well as matters of monitoring, feedback discussion and performance record formed an integral part of the general management of the project. A low-key pragmatic approach to experiment was adopted, allowing inevitably for a degree of failure as well as success. Not surprisingly, implementation demonstrated that sometimes as much is to be learned from 'things going wrong' as from 'things going right'. With the emphasis on the hands-on practical approach appropriate to the site and the circumstance of works in progress, detailed scientific performance appraisal was not possible. Others in the region are now concentrating on this cruial issue.[15]

THE ESSENTIAL PROBLEM OF BUILDING WITH EARTH

The minimum constituents for a mud or daub wall built in the traditional wet-mixed and unshuttered way were water, aggregate and binder. The inert fraction of any earth provides the aggregate, with its clay fraction providing the binder. Aggregates, which are the bulk of the mixture, can, in the case of mud, range in individual particle size from quite large stones through gravel and sand to the finest of silts. This is all held in place by the binder, the clay, which must initially be made wet to coat the aggregates and which is always present in lesser amounts (Fig 21). Ratios of 80%:20% aggregate to clay

have been recorded in Devon (Williams-Ellis 1919 [1947], 36). Recent research in the region suggests that much lower amounts of clay may not be uncommon and this may have been the case at Bowhill, discussed in more detail below.

An understanding of the nature of clay is the key to an understanding of mainstream building technique. Clay holds the aggregate in place mechanically with suction playing an important part during building. It is difficult to use as a binder since it is volumetrically unstable; it expands when wetted and contracts again when dried. Drying contraction in clay produces cracking. Cracks weaken the wall and speed the processes of weathering and decay (Fig 22). Dealing with drying-out shrinkage was thus a major preoccupation for the builder in wet-mixed mud and daub. In this respect, clay-based cob and daub, such as that at Bowhill, must be differentiated from chalk or chalk-and-clay cob and daub, found in some other parts of Britain, where the calcium carbonate element present reduces the effect of shrinkage-cracking.

Traditional practice used three separate but interlinked approaches to combat the shrinkage problem. Firstly,

Figure 21 Cob, the basic ingredients: (from bottom, clockwise) fibre, small stone/gravel, clay, large stone, silt/sand, dung. A sample of Cumbrian material. (Copyright: Ray Harrison)

Figure 22 Close-up detail of an experimental cob wall built without fibre by Alfred Howard, early 1980s. Very heavy cracking is evident as is also a major shrinkage gap away from the door frame (right). (Copyright: Ray Harrison)

clay content in the raw material could be reduced towards the lowest possible level commensurate with it continuing to fulfil its function as the matrix within which the bulking aggregates were held. This was done by adding extra aggregate to a fixed quantity of the basic raw material. (The alternative was to avoid using over-clayey material at all.) A second precaution related to water content. Water has to be added during mixing. It is needed to produce a homogeneous and malleable material capable of being formed into a cohering mass on the wall head. Too much water, however, and the clay element in the mix becomes ungovernable. Thus the builders might strive to keep water content to the practical minimum. The less water initially present, the less subsequent drying shrinkage. Alternatively, if making the cob or daub over-wet was unavoidable, or necessary, the completed mixture might be left some time to 'drain' (or 'firm–up') and lose, and thus better incorporate some of its moisture before use. Thirdly, fibre was added during mixing. Straw was the most commonly used fibre, but there were many alternatives. The presence of straw cannot prevent the formation of cracks but it probably spreads them out, distributing them throughout the wall as hair-line fractures as the clay shrinks. Fibre was added for other reasons as well. It may have assisted drying-out, it helped the material turn over more easily during mixing, hang on the fork and wall during building and it soaked up and then released water during mixing. Im–portantly, as recent experiment has shown, it provided shear resistance in the newly dry cob wall, reinforcing the material under compression.[16] What its effect in this last respect is in ancient walls, such as those at Bowhill, is difficult to say.

It is often said that the building process is a slow one. In fact recent experiment suggests that in terms of traditional building this is not particularly the case. Alfred Howard feels that there is probably little difference in erection speed between lime mortared stone and red Devon cob.[17]

Daub for conventional wattled walling was often thrown onto the armature by hand in order to obtain better adherence than trowelling-on might give. The action is shown, in the illustration of the application of the external daub coating to double-lathed walling at Bowhill (see Fig 9). 'Throwing' seems to have been a deeply ingrained part of the old tradition. The phrase 'here's mud in your eye' refers to the plight of the unfortunate apprentice who, on his initiation into the craft, was not advised to cast his handful of mud in time with that of the master, standing on the opposite side of the wattle. While throwing can be difficult with ceiling daubing, the principle of pressing the material onto or through laths from both sides at the same time still stands. It is, however, less relevant with double lath walling where the wall core itself is filled first by ramming daub in, downwards, from one side. The downward ramming action follows cob construction where the material is generally placed and compressed in horizontal layers, largely from above.

A key difference between mainstream daub and cob is reflected in the differing shrinkage patterns of the completed work. 'Block' shrinkage, mass contraction both horizontally and vertically, tends to be the norm with solid materials such as cob and cob block (unfired earth brick). A shrinkage gap can be seen between block and mould in the example shown (Fig 23), produced as the material dries and contracts on itself. The same effect can be seen, at a much larger scale, in the completed cob cross-wall at Bowhill (Fig 24). Here the mass of the wall has drawn an inch (25mm) and more away from the door frame. In some parts of England, notably the New Forest and Buckinghamshire, mass shrinkage in cob results in more or less vertical cracks quite evenly spaced along the wall within each course of the material. This is probably a sign of a 'strong', ie clayey, material. By contrast a network of small-scale cracks tends to develop with daubs as their contraction is restrained within by their wooden armatures. Figure 25 shows a typical example of such shrinkage cracking, again from new work at Bowhill. In neither case, cob or daub, need such cracks represent a problem; everything is down to circumstance, scale and degree. These are matters which localized building tradition fully accounted for but which we now have to learn over again from the beginning.

When the use of earth was part of mainstream practice, builders understood its strengths and weaknesses and knew that, like other materials, it could be used badly or well. As a result of care and attention, the quality of some of the earth repairs at Bowhill equals anything done there in the past. In some other cases in the building, however, as is inevitable where experiment is concerned, although high standards were still reached and equal care taken, at the end there were lessons to be learnt (Figs 26 and 27).

THE SOILS USED IN BUILDING AT BOWHILL

Material used in earth walling was (wherever possible) taken from close to the site. Archaeological excavation identified Bowhill as having had a cob-walled predecessor.

Figure 23 Bowhill, dry cob block in mould, 1992. Note shrinkage gap and corrugations to top of block resulting from finishing by tamping with the edge of a board.

Figure 24 Bowhill, the new cob cross-wall: mass horizontal shrinkage away from the door-frame, 1993. Note the salts effluorescence (bottom), a danger to plaster.

Figure 25 Bowhill, network shrinkage cracks in new double-lathed daub, 1991.

Figure 26 Section of c 1500 wall-head cob, 1991. Shrinkage of original undamaged cob down and away from eaves-purlin shows as a horizontal gap between top of the cob and underside of the timber, through which light can be seen. Note the inappropriate, pre-1978, 'repairs' in the lower part of the wall.

Figure 27 Section of c 1990 cob showing shrinkage down and away from the eaves- purlin, 1991. Crack under the purlin is greatest where depth of new cob is greatest, ie to right of photograph.

Some of the material from the walls of that building may have found its way into the walls of its successor.

Bowhill is located on soils known as the Crediton series which are described as 'well drained gravelly loams from red Permian breccias and conglomerates'. [18] These are generally well-graded soils, reddish-brown in colour and were widely used for building cob structures in south-east Devon. The subsoils in the immediate vicinity of Bowhill are characterized by their very deep red colour and their relatively good dimensional stability. Linear shrinkage in these soils is normally no more than 1% to 2%. The material used for Bowhill's new cob cross-wall (see below) is considered to be typical of such local sub-soils. It was not specially selected (see below), nor was it analysed at the outset, before use. An assumption was made, that as it was local, it was likely to perform satisfactorily. A sample taken later in the course of the works gave the balance of constituents shown in Table 1.

Table 1: Bowhill soil constituents

Clay	Silt	Sand	Gravel/Stone
15%	22%	42%	21%

Even a linear shrinkage rate of 2% has a significant effect. Bowhill's new cob cross-wall, described below, reduced on drying, over an 11'3" (3.42m) length between door frame and the north wall, by a maximum of $2^{3}/_{8}$" (60mm) ($1^{3}/_{16}$" or 30mm at each end). This gives a rate of about 1.75% linear shrinkage. Similar raw material, sieved of its largest stones, mixed to a stiff consistency with water and placed in a test box and allowed to dry, produced a linear shrinkage rate of over 3%. Shrinkage here was found to be very significantly reduced by the addition of 10% by volume of sand. A 20% extra sand mix showed no great improvement over the 10% mix; however, shrinkage failure points were most evenly distributed with the 20% mix. The test-box arrangements are shown in Figure 28. Further samples of the new walling material, taken randomly, gave the ingredient percentage breakdowns shown in Table 2.

Table 2: Constituents of new walling material, Bowhill

	Clay	Silt	Sand	Gravel/Stone
Site a) new cross wall	18%	38%	17%	27%
Site b) new cross wall (extra sand added)	9%	21%	46%	24%

That a local clay-bound mix, with added sand, containing only 9% clay, appears to perform satisfactorily, in an admittedly non-imposed load-bearing situation, is

Figure 28 Test boxes of dried-out subsoil: top box with no added sand; central box with 10% sand added; lower box with 20% sand added. Degree of shrinkage shows at the ends of boxes and in cracks across the boxes at intervals.

Table 3: Constituents of samples from the original cob walling

	Clay	Silt	Sand	Gravel/Stone
Site a original internal cob wall	3.5%	28.5%	41%	27%
Site b return angle of former west gable	0.7%	30.3%	40%	29%

confirmed by the fact that no difficulty was experienced with the upper levels of the new cob cross-wall (where this 'amended' material was used) either during work or on completion. It is also confirmed by very limited sampling of the original cob walling, in two places only, which produced, according to conventional wisdom, surprising results. The proportion of clay present was found to be very small, much lower than that which would normally be considered desirable for the construction of durable cob walls. Both samples (see Table 3) were taken from the ground-floor west room in the South Range.

Where such small amounts of clay are present its matrix function for the aggregates must be much reduced, yet the walls still stand. It seems likely, in these circumstances, that the intermediate and silt fraction in the mix may assume some of the functions of the clay. However, as noted earlier, silt has very little ability of itself to bind, the result here being a weak cob, weak in the sense of the material's ability to resist the effects of rain and rising damp.

The relative weakness of the original material may perhaps be implied in the disappearance of the west and possibly also the east gables of the South Range at Bowhill. Full gables are the most vulnerable part of mass-walled buildings in the vernacular tradition, having always been a problematical form of construction. Where such tall, rain-attracting cob structures meet their stone plinths (this was at first floor level in the east and at two or three feet, 600–900mm, above ground in the west gables) there is the potential for weakening and collapse through render failure and entry of water. Sandy, silty cobs are likely to fail, in these circumstances, more quickly than heavily clay-bound cobs, a fact suggested by recent research into such problems with the sandy cobs of the Dawlish area.[19]

We have seen that the advantage of a weak cob can be a reduction in shrinkage rates. This is a generally useful trait in building but it becomes of particular value where composite construction occurs, as it does at Bowhill. A case in point is the first-floor south elevation junction of cob and stonework in the South Range. Here though the stonework clearly courses and indents with separate thin beds of cob, there is little evidence of differential shrinkage between stone and cob. It may be that the laying of weak cob in thin courses resulted here in negligible shrinkage.

Nationally there seem to have been two ways of building mud walls, one involving high courses of anything between 2–4' (600–1200mm), the other involving shallow courses often 6" (150mm) or less high. Things are confused to a degree by the fact that the taller courses are themselves often built up in thin layers; however the separate low-course system can sometimes be identified by thin beds of straw showing at the wall face. Such beds do not normally occur within courses in the alternative deep system since with this each layer is melded into the one below as the builder works on the wet materials, one wet layer following immediately on the next. The reason for straw beds between courses is uncertain; in some areas they may simply be a layer spread on the course top to protect it while it hardens, and left in position when the next course is added.

As noted above there was evidence in at least the cob walling of the south and remaining section of west elevation of the South Range at Bowhill for the thin-course approach, suggesting that where a course of stonework ended, work was carried on, to the same course depth, in cob (Fig 29). One advantage of this would be an initial course-drying time quicker for equivalent volumes than for a deep course since much

more of the total surface area of the new cob is exposed to the atmosphere, and hence to drying winds, where the course is shallow. Where the builders were working on the walls of quite a large structure like Bowhill, there may have been appreciable savings in time through the adoption of this approach (Fig 30).

Two further samples of cob, new cob used to rebuild the lean-to at the north end of the Great Hall, were also taken. This work, which had involved rebuilding the whole of the lean-to's west, and part of the east, walls, started in 1984 and was based on surviving remains and archaeological evidence under the unrecorded first-phase works. The cob sampled contained similar amounts of clay, ie 0.5% and 2%, to that found in the original walling. It is said to have been obtained from three sources; the site, local building sites and from a collapsed gable wall at Ide. English Heritage Research and Technical Advisory Division had recommended the use of lime with the raw cob.[20] Percentages of 11.6% and 14.7% lime were found in the samples tested, far more than the percentage of clay present.

The lean-to's west wall was built first. It was discovered that the use of a large proportion of lime caused the material to 'go off' and harden very quickly. In fact, attempts to remove a sample for testing from the lower part of the wall proved very difficult because of the hardness of the material. For the east wall and upper parts of the west wall, the percentage of lime was progressively reduced down to around 1:6 and then 1:12. According to former Regional Superintendent Adam Mackenzie it may have been omitted altogether towards the end of the work.

One sample of original, and four of new, daubs were taken as well as one of historic daub plaster. The original daub was from the double-lath core of the seventeenth-century daub partition between the Great and Inner chambers of the South Range. It was deep red in colour and composed almost entirely of fine material (less than 2mm) so had probably been sieved originally. Its composition was clay (25%), silt (53%), sand (20%) and gravel (2%).

Figure 29 Thin courses in the one remaining section of cob in the west gable wall, Bowhill, 1994. Note the later rubblestone external facing added over the original stone plinth to two-thirds the wall-height, showing where the original cob had become eroded. The method of cutting back and facing decayed cob with stone is still used in places in Devon. Any form of cutting-back obviously weakens the wall.

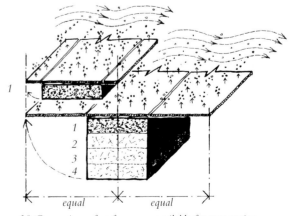

Figure 30 Comparison of surface areas available for evaporation between thin and deep courses. Though one quarter the volume of the deep course, the thin course has half the surface area to dry out from. Mass for mass it will, therefore, harden more quickly than the deep course. Thin course work is not common in Devon. (Pers comm Peter Child)

 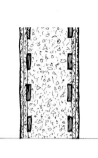

Figure 31 Detail of daub plaster to, and sketch section through, seventeenth-century double-lathed panel, Bowhill, 1990. Note the matted hair visible in the top of the plaster.

Figure 32 Detail of c 1500 integral daub-plastered double-lath panelling between Hall and Great Chamber, 1990. Note small section of lath showing behind the daub. Sketch section through integral daub-plastered double-lathed panelling, Bowhill.

More than three quarters of the mix was made up of clay and silt, the amount of 25% clay contrasting strongly with the minimal amounts apparently present in the original cob walling. The difference in mix balance here probably reflects the construction system. As the daub core was packed down between lathing which was itself to be separately plastered over later, there was no need to worry about shrinkage cracking. The result was a 'strong' panel, parts of which, though only some 4" (100mm) thick, were capable of standing on their own indefinitely as long as no pressure was applied to them. It is uncertain why larger aggregate was removed, as, given the confinement of the core, its retention would not have caused problems. Perhaps a contiguous exterior daub plaster, through and over the laths, was originally intended, in which case removal of the stones makes sense.

A separate daub plaster (Fig 31) applied over this double-lath panelling survived in part and a sample was tested. It consisted of a single piece of 'plaster' in two apparent coats, the inner measuring $5/_{16}$" (8mm) in thickness and the outer $9/_{32}$" (7mm). In both layers the material was reinforced by hair. The colour of the daub was red/brown, with the outer coat slightly darker than the inner coat. Pockets of calcium carbonate were observed in both layers. In the inner coat the amount of

calcium carbonate present by volume was 1:13; in the outer coat it was in the ratio $1:6^{1}/_{2}$. It was present in discrete pockets, possibly as chalk particles. The calcium carbonate content by dry weight in the outer coat was 5%; this is within the range in which it is considered effective, when used to improve the performance of clay. Ninety six per cent of the daub material was in the range of fine sand and downwards. Unfortunately tests did not include establishing silt and clay content. Seven per cent by weight of the inner, and 2% of the outer, layer was animal hair, hence it came to be known as HHD, heavily haired daub. The extra 'chalk' in the outer layer would have offset the lesser amount of hair there.

The texture of this daub plaster closely resembled that of thick felt. The calcium carbonate and the heavy hair reinforcement were included to reduce shrinkage and cracking in such fine particled material. The hair also ensured that the daub spanned the backing laths without the cracking and bond failure that could result from differential movement between materials with different coefficients of expansion, ie between the daub plaster and the oak lathing.

Unfortunately, it did not prove possible to analyse the daub from the original double-lathed partition, between the Great Hall and Great Chamber, where an integral daub plaster had been used (Fig 32).

3　Mixing cob and daub and making cob-blocks

After lunch, the east wing party mixed tons of concrete and laid most of the surface concrete slab. When the aggregate ran out … all were employed on a massive COB STOMP. This was achieved with great chanting accompanying three men with spades moving in a circle while turning the cob and then Alan in the size 11 boots did a war-dance puddle on it. Meanwhile ice creams and tea. Very hot clear day.[21]

MIXING: AN INTRODUCTION

The first aim of mixing, self evidently, is to produce a material that is satisfactory to use. With cob there is an intimate link between the nature of the prepared material and the act of placing it into position on the wall head; from this everything else follows.

The usual convenient minimum labour requirement for a small, traditional, un-shuttered, cob-building operation was two to mix and pass material up, and one to tread down on the wall top. No builder wants to have men standing around; thus the consistency of material forked up to the wall-head had to be such that the man there could pack it down and quickly be ready to receive the next 'clat'.[22] The joint working pace of the men would call for a mix that stayed stiff and upright but that also allowed quick placing without too much effort. Up to a point the moister the material, the easier it would be to compress, but the more difficult it would be to make it retain its shape. A balance had to be struck.

> Great care had to be exercised in not using too much water or a 'slip' is likely to occur, which means the rebuilding of a large portion of the 'lift'… I only remember one 'slip' occurring … for I was water boy, and paid the penalty for being too free with the water (Dibben 1914).

Conversely, the drier the material, and at some point the more fibre in it, the more difficult it is to compress, the more air voids remain within it and the less well it hangs together. As Alfred Howard says 'it gets weak, like dung'.

Traditionally, mixing was a process to be learned, with judgement developing out of working directly with the wet material, since the nature and requirements of the particular soil being prepared become apparent as mixing proceeds. As no two soils are identical in their constituents, so each mixing will vary slightly from the next. Variation will be in the amount of water and fibre needed and possibly in the need to add extra aggregate. In these circumstances taking things gradually by adding water and fibre by degrees makes common sense and is the recommended practice for those starting to learn the techniques. Once the basic management of the material is understood through experience, then short-cuts can be considered. Mixing in cattle-pens or with horses was common. Alfred Howard maintains that four to five tons of wet material can be produced by two bullocks in this way in half an hour. Johnson (1806) describes the use of animals:

> Oxen or horses, the former being preferred on account of the cloven foot, are driven over the [cob] layers as in thrashing; and as the cattle in treading cause it to spread, a labourer with a three-pronged fork throws it up again (Johnson 1806, 78).

Today large-scale mixing using tractors has become popular, as such methods cut down on time and effort considerably. Mini-diggers with crawler tracks have proved particularly useful and efficient.

To judge when cob can be placed it is usual to estimate how much it sticks to the boot (Fig 33). Clearly it is counter-productive if quantities adhere as this will make packing it down hard work. Fibre tends to soak up and then control the spread of water through the material. Should a clay-cob mix continue to be too sticky in spite of every attempt to dry it up, then it may be too 'strong', ie it may contain too much clay, to be useful. In such circumstances extra aggregate, ie sand, gravel etc, may

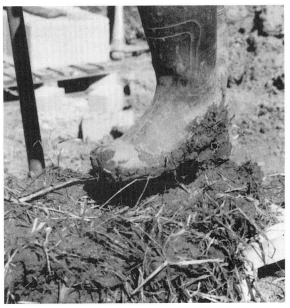

Figure 33 Typical cob consistency, from Alfred Howard's training wall, Bowhill, 1990. (Copyright: Ray Harrison)

be added. This was a traditional solution: pit-gravel in the New Forest, shillet in Cornwall.[23]

It was noted during hand-mixing small amounts at Bowhill that when a gritty sand was added, the change in the nature of the material could be felt through the boot and with small quantities could also be heard in the sound of treading.

Given the particular circumstances at Bowhill the fact that the original material for the new cross-wall (see below) shrank appreciably was not a serious problem. Elsewhere, however, such degrees of contraction might be unacceptable; soils will then need to be sampled and analysed and, if necessary, amended for best performance. The most skilled of today's practitioners will sometimes arrange to mix two separate soils to counter an excess of clay in one of them. Details of manuals dealing with soils testing and analysis can be found in the bibliography.

Tests with conventional drum mixers (cement mixers) at Bowhill confirmed that these can be used to make cob. The process is not entirely straightforward if one is seeking a result similar to that coming from hand-mixing. Wettish, semi-slurried cob can, however, easily be made in a drum mixer. If this route is taken with clay-based material then courses may have to be kept shallow. Larry Keefe's small cob shelter at Starcross near Dawlish was built of a very wet cob, with courses only 9" (225mm) high (Fig 34). Shallow courses of such wet material stay stable during construction, and shrinkage is probably less potentially destructive, than it would be with higher wet-coursed work. The material must be laid and compacted working from the side, being too wet to accept the usual arrangement of a man on top. The example of the work of Kevin McCabe, another innovative modern cob builder, in which a very large amount of initial vertical shrinkage, on deep courses, took place, confirms a wetter

mix than is normal regional practice today, and may be a pointer to further future, local developments. There are in the international literature a number of references to the use of wet cob mixes (notably from Brittany)[24] sometimes placed between boards. Monitored experiment is needed before serious advice on the approach can be safely given.

At a training session arranged at the start of the second stage cob works at Bowhill in the late summer of 1990, Alfred Howard was invited to introduce the English Heritage team to hand-mixing (Fig 35). Some records speak of the over-wintering of the new material before mixing ('generally it was left to weather through the winter', Oliver 1949, 37) but Alfred Howard does not subscribe to the need for this. Nonetheless it is a process that can do no serious harm, if time allows, assuming work is to start in the spring.

The two raw subsoil heaps at Bowhill had been there for a while and had hardened, drying out during 1990. Pick-axes were then needed to break out the material, which came away in large lumps needing further breaking down. This initial supply came from two demolished houses, one nearby and another in Dunsford village further down the road. The practice of reusing sub-soil from derelict structures was noted in 1641 by Henry Best, East Yorkshire farmer and diarist.[25] Later on in the progress of the works further subsoil was brought in from

Figure 34 Building with wet cob, Starcross, Devon. (Copyright: P Trotman/BRE)

Figure 35 Alfred Howard's team preparing cob and building the bus-shelter, Down St Mary, Devon. (Copyright: Crediton Courier 1980)

the excavations for a reservoir some 300 or 400 yards away from the site.

For the production of the small amounts of material required for the training session, a heap of between four (1.2 m) and six feet (1.8 m) in diameter was needed. Such a heap is a point of continuous output, dry, unmixed material replenishing that prepared and taken to the wall. It is a convenient size for two men to trample, while, if labour is plentiful, a third, and perhaps a fourth, keeps them supplied with dry soil and water, and help turn the heap and move it when the time comes. Clough Williams Ellis's description from *c* 1920 remains the standard, if brief, reference.

A 'bed' of clay-shale is formed close to the wall where it is to be used, sufficient to do one perch. A perch is a superficial measurement described as 16½ ft

long, 1 ft high, and the amount of material will vary according to the thickness of the wall required. Four men usually work together. The big stones are picked out. (They can also be kicked out). The material is arranged in a circular heap about five or six feet in diameter.

Starting at the edge the men turn over the material with cob picks, standing and treading on the material all the time. One sprinkles on water and another sprinkles on barley straw from a wisp under his left arm. The heap is then turned over again in the other direction, treading continuing all the time. 'Twice turning' is usually considered sufficient (Williams-Ellis 1919 [1947], 37).

Cob picks were special, purpose-made flat-tined trident forks (Fig 36). 'Twice turning' was still the way 60 years

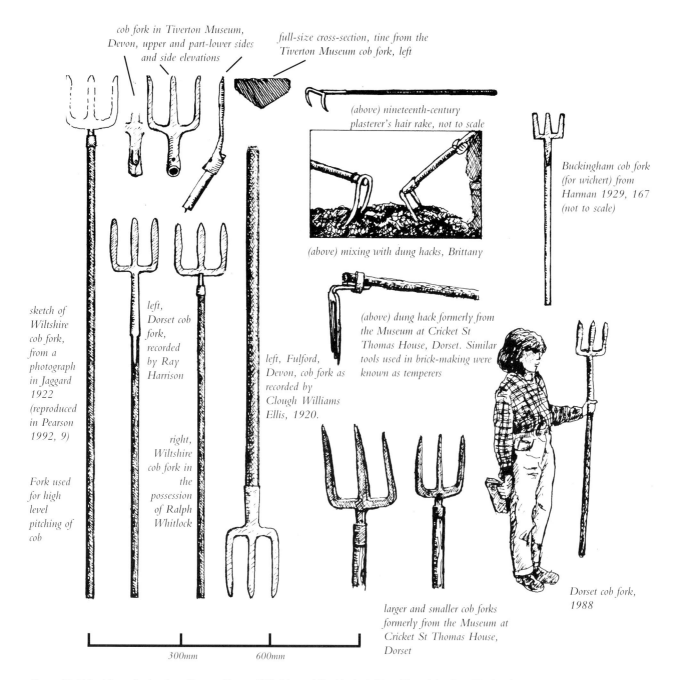

cob fork in Tiverton Museum, Devon, upper and part-lower sides and side elevations

full-size cross-section, tine from the Tiverton Museum cob fork, left

(above) nineteenth-century plasterer's hair rake, not to scale

(above) mixing with dung hacks, Brittany

Buckingham cob fork (for wichert) from Harman 1929, 167 (not to scale)

sketch of Wiltshire cob fork, from a photograph in Jaggard 1922 (reproduced in Pearson 1992, 9)

Fork used for high level pitching of cob

left, Dorset cob fork, recorded by Ray Harrison

right, Wiltshire cob fork in the possession of Ralph Whitlock

left, Fulford, Devon, cob fork as recorded by Clough Williams Ellis, 1920.

(above) dung hack formerly from the Museum at Cricket St Thomas House, Dorset. Similar tools used in brick-making were known as temperers

larger and smaller cob forks formerly from the Museum at Cricket St Thomas House, Dorset

Dorset cob fork, 1988

300mm   600mm

Figure 36 Cob-picks and rakes from Devon, Dorset, Wiltshire and Buckinghamshire. (Copyright: Ray Harrison)

later when Alfred Howard built his bus shelter and is probably a reflection of the good cob-making qualities of Devon soils. Some soils outside the region may need more attention. The nineteenth-century Essex clay-dauber's joke that 'you spoil it if you tread it too much' carries the suggestion of a rather longer mixing process (Hill 1843, 359).

The spot upon which mixing takes place ought ideally to be hardened or cleared of topsoil in some way. Although Alfred Howard says that a bit of topsoil won't hurt, best practice is to avoid it where possible. The working base at Bowhill appeared to be subsoil mixed with some hoggin, still a relatively absorbent surface. (Hoggin is small stone, 'bound' in a coating of loam, as it comes from the pit. For a detailed nineteenth-century description of hoggin and its use see Law 1855, 100.)

When cob was being prepared in this traditional way which might best be described as 'controlled water' foot mixing, it was found that if there was any danger of rain then it was wise to stop mixing and cover the heap. This is because uncontrolled water content during mixing disrupts quality control. Following this realization the mixing process at Bowhill always took place under cover (Fig 37). It was also found that protecting the soil heap from rain with a tarpaulin allowed water content to be properly adjusted as mixing went on.

In apparent contrast to what little we know of recent practice in Devon, documentary information on former national tradition contains scattered references to 'soaking' the material.[26] This is common international practice. Heavily watering the raw material (leaving it to soak in shallow pits) to break down the clay fraction is an alternative to controlled-water mixing, but care has to be taken that in the end the silt and clay are properly distributed through the aggregates. The latter will of course fall to the bottom of any mixture where there is enough water to put the silt and clay into suspension. The completed wet mix may need to stand before use, unlike the controlled-water mix which if carefully prepared may be used immediately.

Another way of breaking down and spreading out the clay element is by crushing the soil in a fully dry condition. Removal of large stones followed by stamping and beating before mixing can produce a dry, even tilth which mixes quickly and easily for daub. This approach, convenient where small amounts of material are needed quickly, was found to work satisfactorily at Bowhill.

Although heavy watering of the raw soil is not part of the tradition perpetuated by Alfred Howard, he supports the idea of leaving the prepared material to 'prove' for a short period before use, especially when machine mixing is involved. The Bowhill workers observed that 'proving' helps to cure and soften the straw in the mix.

The comment above is quoted from the masons, or the labourers associated with them, who carried out all the cob, daub, plastering and rendering works at the site. Their assumption of these roles is very much in the tradition of the old DEL teams. For this reason, some of the fine detail of what is described below can be seen as having developed from the stone-laying/mortar-using tradition. In Buckinghamshire, so Walter Rose tells us, the makers of the local mud walls were latterly known as 'masoners' (Rose 1987, 101). They worked, of course, with both stone and 'wichert'.

HAND-MIXING AT BOWHILL

The process of mixing demonstrated by Alfred Howard at Bowhill varied little between material for cob or daub. Significant differences lie in the fibre he recommended: straw for cob and more pliable hay for daub, and in the removal of gravel and stones for the thinner varieties of daub such as that at Bowhill (see Chapter 2). Aggregate removal was done by 'screening', a tedious job if the soil is damp and which results in a mix where clay content is higher, in percentage terms, than in the original soil. Account may need to be taken of this if there is any anxiety about shrinkage in the finished wall.

Typical stages identified in the mixing process are as follows (the sequence may vary but the principles stand):

- Wet the ground where mixing is to be done.
- Spread over this a thin layer of uncut (in this case combined barley) straw or hay.
- Sprinkle with water.
- Shovel on a thin layer of broken sub-soil from the heap, with a maximum loose thickness of perhaps 2"–3" (50–75mm).
- Add a further scatter of fibre and a dash of water.
- Tread. This involves attempting to reduce the heap to the point where the boots penetrate the mass fully. 'Heeling', standing on one's heels, is an efficient and traditional way of doing this.

Figure 37 Covered mixing area in the courtyard, Bowhill, 1991. Cob being lifted by bucket to works area at first floor, South Range.

Figure 38 Cob treading completed, 1990. (Copyright: Ray Harrison)

- Add more water, soil and fibre in small amounts as mixing proceeds, building the mass up gradually. It ought not to become so thick that those treading are left working at the surface layers rather than getting deep into the material.
- When the maximum workable depth is reached and the mass appears well mixed, turn the heap over. Because of suction and the mass weight of the wet cob, it will only be possible to turn it in small amounts at a time, this in itself assisting mixing. It should immediately be apparent that the underside of the heap is still partially dry.
- After forming the new heap, continue treading, lesser amounts of straw and water only being added if necessary, until the whole is judged ready for use (Fig 38). If very wet patches appear, these may be dried up by throwing on small amounts of dry subsoil.

An alternative approach tried by the DEL team and found to work satisfactorily was to dry-mix most of the soil and straw in a batch, and then add water and tread. The sequence was as follows:

- The heap was built up in three stages, each made up of two layers: first, proportionally, a bucket of compressed straw and second two buckets of soil.
- The whole was then turned dry using pitchforks.
- Following this it was trodden and heeled and water was added in small amounts at a time as this went on. A final measure of soil was added during this process.
- The whole heap was then turned onto a new spot and trodden again.
- This was repeated for a final time before the material was ready for use.

It will be noted that this approach, with its thicker beds, required an extra turn. It is revealing to compare this particular method, arrived at empirically by the works

staff at Bowhill, with Johnson's description of mixing, using animals, from nearly 200 years before:

> [The soil] is generally thrown into a pile, and therefrom a layer is spread in a circle round the bottom of it; on the top of which circle is spread some hay or straw, about 3, 4 or 5 inches long, previously soaked in water; the whole is then sprinkled with water from a pan, or thrown on with a scoop; another layer of soil, hay and water and sometimes a third are laid on the first, and then oxen or horses [the former preferred because of the cloven hoof] are driven over the layers as in threshing (Johnson 1806, 78).

The material shown in Figure 39 is a good indication of the consistency of cob preferred by the masons at Bowhill.

Figure 39 The first course of the new cob cross-wall. The mixing box in the foreground contains cob ready for use. Frank Lawrence at the box, Tom Perring placing cob, using a mallet, 1991. The material in Frank Lawrence's hand gives an idea of the consistency sought by the masons.

FIBRE

In the modern mixing processes described above there is no recommendation for chopped or soaked fibre. This follows what is recorded of mainstream tradition in the west which has it that although the straw was sometimes chopped, usually it was 'merely pulled abroad and bruised with the hands' (Laycock 1920, 179). Only one British commentator argues that chopped straw was preferred because it was 'easier to handle'.[27] In practice the uncut straw in the cob at Bowhill did not appear to impede mixing, or subsequent use (Fig 40). Similarly, the uncut hay used in the daub panels posed no problem in use. However, where very thin daub is used for 'dubbing out' in layers, then chopped fibre seems to have been common

Figure 40 Long straw for cob, Bowhill. Mark Joy mixing, 1990.

Figure 41 Cut hay for daub; note the Western British 'Devon' shovel and facsimile cob-pick, Bowhill. (Copyright: Ray Harrison)

Figure 42 The Great Hall, Bowhill, looking north: inside mixing for daub to upper partition between Great Hall and Great Chamber; raw soil (top); large mixing box (centre); platform for daub storage (bottom).

nationally and was therefore employed for such work at Bowhill (Fig 41). There could be an advantage in having pre-soaked fibre in the case of layered dry soil-mixes. As noted earlier, fibre will both soak up and release water during mixing. However it was the Bowhill masons' view that dry fibre is easier to mix-in than wet fibre, when mixing conventionally. British references to the pre-soaking of fibre before use are very rare.

It was mentioned earlier that recent tests have confirmed the binding function of fibre in new cob.[28] This is the traditional view of its role and, in this respect, long fibres may have advantages over short ones. It may be noted also that Alfred Howard is critical of modern straw, considering that it is left on the stalk too long, and is therefore more brittle, and less strong, than in the past. Nitrates can weaken it, and it is also crushed by mechanical harvesters. The record indicates that traditional national preference was actually for barley straw. Uncut barley straw presumably had the advantages of 'softness' for mixing, handling and placing, while remaining 'tough' when laid in the walling.

HAND-MIXING INSIDE

For repair work there may be times when it is convenient to mix inside. An experimental box was made up for this purpose at Bowhill. It was constructed from an 8' x 4' (2.4m x 1.2m) sheet of shuttering ply as the base with scaffold boards fixed around the edges to contain the mix (Fig 42). Initially it was lined with heavy-duty polythene sheeting but this was dispensed with after a time, as it prevented any material left in the box from 'breathing', causing its undersurface to sweat.

If full turning of the heap, as one mass, is intended in such a tight space, then only a small amount of material can be prepared at a time. If the heap is turned and trodden by small stages, then the space can be more fully used and this in fact became the practice at Bowhill. The box proved its worth for the hand-completion of mixing already partly done by machine (see below). A half-size box, 4' by 4' (1.2m x 1.2m), was developed by staff for use on the scaffold, for 'knocking-up' cob before placing it in the wall. It was also useful for final treading of material prepared for earth blocks where those were being made in small numbers (see Fig 39).

MACHINE-MIXING

Because of the general scale of the works, rather fragmented working practice and limited amount of space on site, the machines chosen for cob and daub preparation were revolving-drum ('cement') mixers (Fig 43). These allowed mixing teams to be reduced to one, or at most two, workers and called for little more space than did hand-mixing. Production rates were probably higher as well.

With the axis of the drum tilted slightly back from the horizontal as for conventional concrete or mortar mixing, and with a controlled-water mix, added in stages, the local red soil and straw mix clogged the drum's paddles. With the drum axis re-set at the horizontal or even tipped forward slightly, partly mixed soil was carried round the drum to fall from above, in lumps, onto the paddle edges. As this went on, balls of cob quickly appeared; these once formed did not easily reduce further and were tipped out (Fig 44). This experience exactly repeats that of John Deal

Figure 43 Mixing outside: mixing box with section of stock-piled cob at end nearest camera. Frank Lawrence loading the machine, 1991.

Figure 44 Cob-balls tipped out into the mixing box, 1991.

Figure 45 Treading out the balls, 1991.

Figure 46 General view of treading-out following mechanical mixing. Note that the box end behind Frank Lawrence is filled with prepared material. Eventually the whole box is filled, 1991.

ARIBA, some 25 years before. The problem at Bowhill was that although having a similar exterior consistency to controlled hand-mixed cob, the centres of the cob-balls remained relatively dry, the material there being only partially mixed and incorporated.

To overcome this difficulty of unequal mixing, the Bowhill masons arrived at a hybrid arrangement involving machine-mixing and some hand-mixing. The revolving drum was loaded with a shovelful or two of soil and this was heavily slurried in the drum with water. The usual additives of more loose soil, fibre and water were then added in small amounts at a time, the drum continuing to revolve. The whole was a good deal wetter than for a controlled mix. Balls again formed, this time externally wetter than before. These were then tipped out again and trodden (Fig 45), a very brief operation, in which the wet outer part of the balls was melded with their drier interiors. The resulting material was then left for 24 hours to firm-up and for the fibre to soften (Fig 46). It was then 'knocked-up' by treading on the scaffold in small amounts in the small mixing-box immediately before use.

In contrast to this approach was that adopted by Larry Keefe for his 1991 cob-walled shelter at Starcross near Exeter. For this, the material was drum-mixed very wet and consequently did not form into balls at all. When tipped-out it was highly plastic and was immediately placed on the wall head. But as noted before, course-height had to be restricted to no more than 9" (225mm). Interestingly, with very favourable weather conditions, work at Starcross was able to proceed at a rate of one course every two or three days.

The key lesson to be learnt from experience at Bowhill and other sites in Devon in the last few years is that, as far as mixing is concerned, the limits of the local material can usually be overcome in one way or another.

QUANTITIES

The results of some measurements made by planning foreman Tom Williams, in late 1990, early in the works when mixing expertise was still being developed, are included here as a general pointer to the nature of the material. The measurements are specific to the batch of local red subsoil used. The rule of thumb volumetric ratio of soil to fibre was here found to be 6 or 7 to 1. This was on the basis of the fibre being taken from the bale and hand-compressed back into a standard measure, a builder's bucket. One cubic metre of the wet mix (which was eventually left to cure overnight before use) weighed approximately two tonnes. To make one wet cubic metre involved some 161 buckets of soil to 23 buckets of straw. Water content was not recorded but this, combined with straw, seems only to have been about 3.5% or so of the total weight.

BLOCK-MAKING

There was no historic precedent for the use of cob-blocks at Bowhill. They seem never to have been part of West

Country tradition though late isolated examples are known from Thorverton near Exeter, used to brick internal nogged partitions.[29]

The general decision to use cob-blocks arose from the Inspector's wish to repair earth walling as near like-with-like as possible in situations where, as we shall see, the employment of cob was not realistic. Blocks were used in a number of different locations through the building, to be discussed below under the individual repair/reinstatement case studies.

Controlled-water mixes were used throughout, the relative stiffness of the material calling for ramming and punning in the moulds. The cob was nothing like plastic enough to allow it to be thrown in, as in classic brick-making practice, though in a contemporary experimental repair at Sandleholme Pottery in the New Forest, this was achieved. Making the blocks was done entirely by hand, which was acceptable since only relatively small quantities were required at a time. Initially a three-gang closed-bottom mould was used, with holes in the base to help to push the completed blocks out (Fig 47). Builder Kevin McCabe, who became involved in mass production, later developed an eight-gang mould on the same principle, in which he wet-moulded cob bricks. This was made of open compartments fixed to a scaffold plank. The mould bases were lined with polythene, quickly filled with a wet mix and turned over to deposit the soft blocks on the ground. Note the relatively thin depth of McCabe's blocks, helping to offset the fact that, in principle, wet-moulded blocks will take longer to dry than controlled-water mixed blocks (Fig 48). Traditional, ie early nineteenth-century, Norfolk 'clay-lump' manufacturing technique uses a similar wet-moulding system but with fully open moulds. Chalk is often an important consituent in Norfolk block and helps them stiffen more quickly than their clay-only equivalents.[30]

Figure 47 The first cob blocks made at Bowhill showing 3-gang fixed-base mould with release holes below, 1992. The moulding process is slower than for the wet blocks shown in Figure 48.

Figure 48 Builder Kevin McCabe's wet-moulded blocks, at a site near Honiton, Devon, 1993. The mould system is the same as in Figure 47, but release was straightforward because of the wet consistency of the blocks. Wet-moulded blocks are the more usual international form. (Copyright: Ray Harrison)

Problems over extracting the rammed blocks from fixed base moulds caused staff at Bowhill to develop a demountable gang mould. On completion of moulding this was disassembled around the block, leaving the latter standing on the ground, and then reassembled for the next batch (Figs 49, 50 and 51). Because of their method of manufacture the masons found that the blocks tended to delaminate if laid on their edges rather than on their beds, as with stone work (pers comm Charles Smith); see Figure 52.

Figure 49 Ramming cob in a two-gang disassemblable open based mould (open base as in East Anglian tradition), Bowhill 1993.

Figure 51 Disassembling the mould, 1993.

Figure 50 Planing-off surplus cob in the filled mould, 1993.

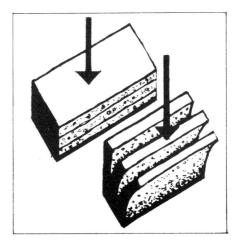

Figure 52 Principle of the effect of laying the Bowhill blocks on their beds or on their bed edges, resulting from the method of ramming the blocks in layers.

Figure 55 Cob-blocks set out to dry inside the Parlour at Bowhill. In the foreground, cob-block moulds disassembled, and cranked and straight sticks for ramming in the moulds, 1993.

Figure 53 Alfred Howard in his workshop at Down St Mary, Devon, demonstrating hand cob-block manufacture in his elderly concrete-block making machine, 1994.

In the case of one large-scale reinstatement, cob-blocks were supplied to the works under contract by Alfred Howard. These were made in an old hand-operated concrete-block machine, producing one block at a time (Fig 53). The cob was first vibrated in the mould using a hand-held electric vibrator. Where blocks are likely to be cut, it is important that large stones be removed from the mix; one advantage of the hand-labour process used at Bowhill is that this aspect of quality control becomes automatic practice. The machine-pressed blocks had to be made with chopped straw; the Bowhill masons considered their hand-made blocks stronger because the straw in them was left uncut. It will be noted that Alfred Howard had adequate arrangements for drying his blocks. These were placed outside, spaced out so that the air could get to them, but protected from rain and sun (Fig 54). At Bowhill, because numbers of blocks were produced over the winter and had to be kept within the building for protection, drying rates were slow (Fig 55).

Figure 54 Alfred Howard's workshop, Down St Mary, Devon, showing left to right, cob wall surrounding concrete 'bullock pen' hard-standing for mixing cob on, cob and timber-framed workshop and cob-blocks for Bowhill, stacked to dry outside, 1994.

4   Building the new cob cross-wall

After the first 'lift', the builder stands on top of the wall to build the next one ... the clay being passed up to him from the ground, each working in harmony with the other, the one on the ground usually putting his prongful of clay onto the builder's prong, which was laid flat, ready to receive it

(Dibben 1914).

BUILDING IN COB AT BOWHILL: BACKGROUND

Most descriptions of cob wall building in Devon are relatively late in date, put down at a time when the tradition was very much in decline. The earliest so far discovered, thought to be that by Tristram Risdon, from 1630, is tantalisingly brief but still confirms a key part of the process, the need for 'rests' in building.

> The Cob, as 'tis call'd, is a Composition of Earth and Straw ... and after a Wall made therewith is rais'd to a certain Height, it is allow'd some Time to Settle before more is laid on [sic] (Risdon 1785 [1970], 50).

Johnson's 1806 record referred to earlier is unique regionally in being taken when building in cob was still in full swing and in its attention to particular details, the part 'beating' can play in the laying-down of the material and the use of the purpose made cob-fork. Johnson speaks from close personal observation when he notes that when the cattle cause the cob to spread in mixing,

> a labourer with a three pronged fork throws it up again ... [the fork prongs are] somewhat flatted ... The labourer takes his fork, and after striking the soil therewith, until it lies like a cake, he takes it up with the fork, and lays in on the wall, striking it there repeatedly at top and sides, until he has packed it close; and proceeds in this way ... trimming off the sides as he goes along ... if the wall is long enough, or the building of a competent size, one part will become sufficiently dry while another is building (Johnson 1806, 78–9).

In the early 1980s at a cob demonstration day for members of the SPAB at his timber yard at Morchard Road, Alfred Howard could be observed with his hay fork, 'striking the soil ... until it lies like a cake' on the ground, exactly as described by Johnson 180 years before. The remarkable continuity of technique here certainly represents best practice, 'Rolls Royce' practice subse-

quently dispensed with at times by modern practitioners for run-of-the-mill work. Revealingly it is also a technique spontaneously reinvented by the Bowhill masons, some of whom flattened prepared material to an even thickness, cut this up into rectangular tiles or 'cakes' and placed each of these individually on the wall before stamping it home. All the actions so carefully documented by Johnson lend to compression of the material, through the driving out of air voids, an important factor in the making of a strong wall.

Johnson makes no mention of treading down the material on the wall-head, the operation that will generally have been central to the process (Fig 56). As noted earlier, in some circumstances cob can be compacted working from the side alone. This was the method used in Gordon Pearson's 1983 rebuilding of the 18" (450mm) thick chalk-mud boundary wall at Andover, and also in Larry Keefe's 1992 cob park-shelter at Starcross in Devon. In both cases shallow course heights meant that satisfactory compression could be obtained by beating only.

Beating, which (as well as compressing from above) knocks back the cob where it overhangs raggedly at the edges as it is laid, can be accomplished by means of the

Figure 56 Down St Mary 1991, treading cob on the wall of Alfred Howard's cob extension, in the traditional way. (Copyright: Ray Harrison)

Figure 57 Bowhill, keeping the side of the wall true by beating-in with the boot, 1991.

Figure 58 (above) Bowhill training day; the effect of beating at the side of the wall. The long straw ends are subsumed into the body of the wall (upper section). Where unbeaten they remain (below) to disguise the wall-face, 1990. (Copyright: Ray Harrison)

Figure 59 Mallet and ramming stick on the new cross-wall, 1991.

Figure 61 Beater used at Trusham, Devon, 1992.

Figure 60 (left) Matthew Vincent, then assistant to Alfred Howard, using a long-handled beater, Bowhill training day, 1990. (Copyright: Ray Harrison)

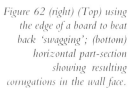

Figure 62 (right) (Top) using the edge of a board to beat back 'swagging'; (bottom) horizontal part-section showing resulting corrugations in the wall face.

flat of the fork, or from above by the heel or side of the boot (Fig 57). The resulting rough squaring up helps to ensure that the worker continues to build true, for it enables him to see where he is going (Fig 58). For packing material into small voids and awkward corners, the masons at Bowhill used wooden mallets and short square-ended wooden ramming sticks (Fig 59). These were, effectively, developed on site. Other tools used for beating also tend to be improvised (Figs 60 and 61). Where a wall being built by Alfred Howard 'swagged' out of true before hardening, this was beaten back to the vertical with the edge of a board, giving a corrugated effect. Again, this is a traditional technique in Devon (Fig 62).

A description in *Country Life* in 1918, one of a number from Johnson onward, confirms the preference of the builders to get on top of the wall and also the continuing use of the cob fork. The worker, it is said,

> lifts the mixture with the pick onto the wall where it is laid and trodden by the builder. The heels should be well used. The more it is trodden the better the cob ... The cob should be laid and trodden in diagonal layers ... This is to secure proper bonding. The cob pick with which the cob is mixed and lifted up to the builder is a three-pronged iron fork slightly curved like a hay fork (anon 1918, 568).

This is the only known report (but repeated by Clough Williams-Ellis) of diagonal layering. Cob seems usually to have been placed horizontally. Diagonal layering was a feature of north European peat- and turf-block building while herringbone masonry has an exceptionally long pedigree, still being used in dry-stone walling and banking in the west today. It is a good way of readily ensuring close compression and was tried out at Bowhill in the new cross-wall, discussed below. That experiment demonstrated that if downward compression is a concern, diagonal layering calls for the expenditure of considerable extra energy when placing material. This is because treading must be done against a slope of material rather

Figure 63 Treading a diagonal ramp: Bowhill new cross-wall, 1991.

than on a bed beneath the feet (Fig 63). The latter method was therefore favoured by the Bowhill masons.

The records often refer to course height. One has it that 'the first rise ... is about four feet, the next not so high, and so every succeeding rise is diminished' (Loudon 1836, 417). Another notes that the cob 'is placed ... to the height of four or five feet' (Collyns 1857, 258). By contrast others state that the cob 'owing to its softness,

Figure 64 Matthew Vincent on top of the tall first course, Alfred Howard's cob extension, Down St Mary. (Copyright: Ray Harrison)

must not be built higher than two feet or a little more' (Hutchinson 1890, 166–7) and 'the ... course ... should not exceed two foot in depth, preferably 1 foot 6 inches' (anon 1918, 568). It seems likely that what is reported here is the use of differing cob mixes of differing wet consistencies. The possible advantages of the much shallower course have already been explored in Chapter 2.

Where tall courses can be achieved, maximum course height will have tended to be that easily reached by a man forking up cob directly from the ground. Including the stone plinth, this might be taken as around 6' (1.8m); 2' or 3' (0.6–0.9m) of masonry plinth and 3' or 4' (0.9–1.2m) of cob, as in Alfred Howard's first 'rise' in his cob extension at Down St Mary (Fig 64). Staging is preferred above this level although as Jaggard's famous photograph of Avebury chalk-mud wallers shows (Pearson 1992, 9), material might be hand-pitched much higher (see Fig 36). The action involved must have been akin to that of pitch-forking straw up a rick or up onto a cart.

THE NEW COB CROSS-WALL: FORM AND LOCATION

The first, and major, piece of new, second stage, cob construction at Bowhill was the reinstatement of the very substantial missing cob cross-wall at the first floor within the South Range between the Oriel and Inner chambers (see Figs 65, 66 and 67). All the evidence needed for the accurate reconstruction of its external form existed within the building. The equivalent missing section of ground floor, stone walling, off which the new cob was to be built, had already been reinstated during the first stages of reconstruction. The Inspector determined on the further reinstatement in order to return this part of the building from one large recently formed space back to its original two, quite architecturally different, rooms. The new structure, built off the new, storey-height, stone ground-floor wall, eventually consisted of ten courses of cob topped by a panel of cob-block, to a height at the ridge of 18'6" (5.63m), and over a width of 16'0" (4.8m). Wall thickness was 30" (0.76m) at base tapering on one side above head height, to a minimum at the ridge, of 18" (0.45m) A doorway was incorporated at one side against the south wall of the range.

Three main technical issues were faced in building the cross-wall: the attaching of its ends to the existing external walls, the incorporation of the doorway and the management of the triangular wall peak.

Fixings to cob: pegs and lintels

It is not physically easy to join substantial amounts of old and new cob where these abut at right angles. Inevitable downward drying shrinkage in the new work may tear attempts at a permanent, structural, bond; this is much better made, if at all, after the new work has settled. At Bowhill, because structural continuity was unnecessary, the new work was simply vertically, and permanently, aligned against the old by means of a timber shear-key. This was face-pegged to the existing cob north wall on the

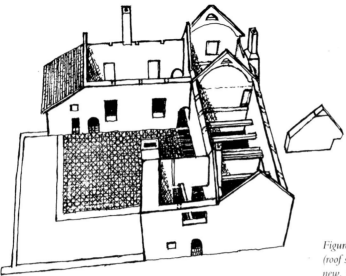

Figure 65 Location of new cob cross-wall – first floor, South Range (roof structure omitted for clarity). Form of new wall and location of new, fixed, door-frame shown to right of illustration.

Figure 66 Location of new cob cross-wall. Original wall scar is visible (left) immediately in front of the first jointed-cruck truss, 1990.

Figure 67 Shear key pegged to centre of scar of original cob cross-wall, 1990.

new wall's centre line. The method was well demonstrated by Alfred Howard in his works at Down St Mary. The new cob locks around the key and in drying can slide freely down against it (Fig 68).

The square-section oak shear-key was pegged to the existing wall in four places. Holes were pre-drilled into the cob without difficulty and the oak pegs were then tapped gently home, through the key (Fig 67). Pre-drilling of hardened cob is sensible with such works. Driving pegs to any depth without this precaution may split the cob, though for smaller shallower depth fixings, this was common practice.

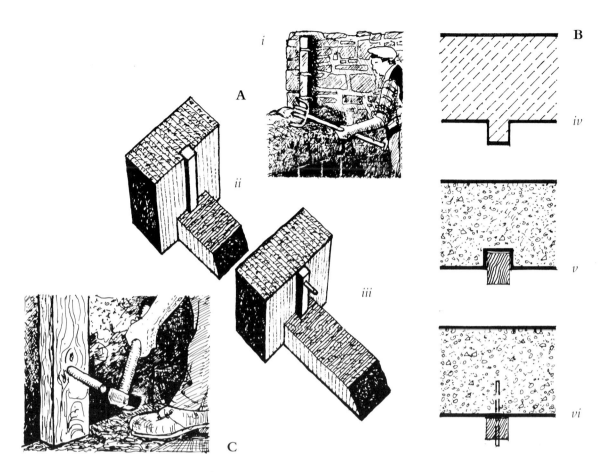

Figure 68 Shear keys; (A) types of shear key: (i) integral stone key, Down St Mary, (ii) recessed loose-fitted timber key, (iii) pegged timber key; (B) plans of shear-key types: (iv) integral stone key, (v) recessed loose-fitted timber key, (vi) pegged timber key; (C) driving peg to fix foot of shear-key, Bowhill (after a photograph by D Garner).

By contrast, heavy pegs can be easily driven into damp cob during the building process. All the oak plates at the wall top of Alfred Howard's cob house extension at Down St Mary (see Fig 19) were pegged in this way as were the fixing grounds to the window reveals. Traditionally, lintels, like fixing grounds, were generally built in loose as the wall rose, the rational approach, adopted by Alfred Howard, being to fit the windows and doors with their fixed vertical dimensions after the wall had settled. Note the 'trestle pieces' spreading the load at each side of the opening in Figure 69. These are certainly part of nineteenth-century Devon tradition. How much further back their use goes is uncertain. At Bowhill lintel ends rest directly on the cob as does the foot of one of the jointed crucks.[31]

The doorway through the new cross-wall [32]

Dealing with the doorway required in the new cross-wall posed the second problem of differential shrinkage. Because it had to be tight against the existing south wall, its lintel would bed at one end into fixed material. At the other end it would rest in wet cob, which would tend to shrink downwards as it dried. The lintel would thus

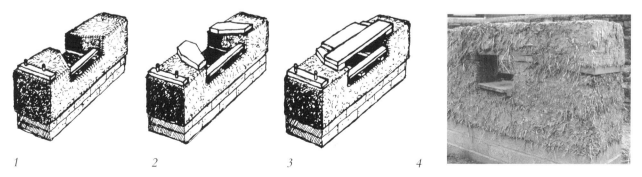

Figure 69 Bowhill training day: Alfred Howard's demonstration wall section: (1) left, door fixing-ground held down by two pegs; centre, window embrasure with cill-fixing grounds; (2) trestle-pieces added to course top to each side of embrasure; (3) lintels placed over embrasure, resting on trestle pieces; (4) the section of wall illustrated in sketches (1) to (3) with a further course of cob laid over the door fixing-ground and window embrasure, 1990.

Figure 70 (left) Alfred Howard's extension, Down St Mary, structural crack developed as a result of unequal vertical shrinkage onto and beside a stone pier.

Figure 71 (right) Fixed door frame in position, cob cross-wall under construction (right), 1991.

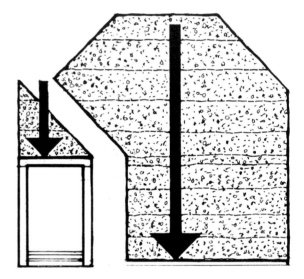

Figure 72 Diagram of Bowhill cross-wall showing differing potential amounts of vertical shrinkage, fixed door-frame and diagonal slip or shear plane.

eventually drop at one end. This in turn would fracture the new walling where it extended over the lintel (Fig 70). The solution attempted was a fixed door frame with jambs and lintel in one self-supporting structure (Fig 71). To avoid the differential upward shrinkage crack that must develop at the upper corner of the frame (Fig 72), a diagonal shear- or slip-plane was arranged through the new cob work, above the door. This took the form of a sloping bed of straw intended to completely divorce a triangular wedge of new cob, seated on the door-frame top, from the rest of the new wall (Figs 73 and 74). This, it was hoped, would allow the two areas of new wall to slide against each other as they dried out and settled differentially. The details of the arrangements are best studied in the illustrations (Figs 73 and 74). In the event (and to date) fracturing of the cob at the door frame corner was limited at most to a vestigial 6" (150mm) long diagonal crack showing on one side only of the wall. Figure 75 shows the completed, fully-dried, joint. Part of the intention of this experiment, successfully achieved, had been to show that stability need not be compromised by the effective separation of abutting sections of walling.

Building the cross-wall

Wall building commenced after the filling with new, carefully rammed, cob, of a low-level hole in the existing cob adjoining the base of the shear key, the fitting of the shear key and the erection of the door frame. The top of the stone ground floor cross-wall formed the base of the new work. This was sprayed-up with water as was the existing cob walling around the shear key to prevent sudden loss of moisture from the new cob into the drier existing fabric.[33]

Courses were trodden in a series of thin, successive, horizontal layers each 4"–6" (100–150mm) deep and course-depth in the lower part of the wall was kept down to about 1' 6" (0.45m) on a wall thickness of 2' 6" (0.76m). This was largely a matter of caution over the performance of the material; at upper levels, with increased confidence, course depths were increased, this in conjunction with limited experiments with shuttering. Alfred Howard stresses the importance of keeping each side of the course up above the centre of the wall to ensure a true face line. Furthermore, if the wall centre rises more quickly than its sides, though structurally not a problem,

Figure 73 Slip-plane with straw isolating-layer in place. The vertical projecting laths in front of the extended door-jamb tenons were intended for withdrawal, see below, Fig 74, 1992.

Figure 75 The completed detail.

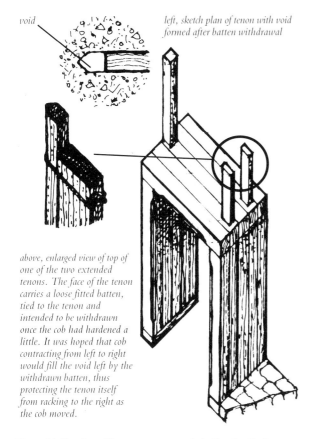

void

left, sketch plan of tenon with void formed after batten withdrawal

above, enlarged view of top of one of the two extended tenons. The face of the tenon carries a loose fitted batten, tied to the tenon and intended to be withdrawn once the cob had hardened a little. It was hoped that cob contracting from left to right would fill the void left by the withdrawn batten, thus protecting the tenon itself from racking to the right as the cob moved.

Figure 74 Sketches of frame arrangement including detail of withdrawable batten. The extended tenons were intended to lock the frame and the cob above it, together. In spite of the shrinkage space allowed, horizontal movement in the drying wall still distorted the door frame a little, racking the top sideways.

a round-topped course cross-section results, an unsatisfactory working surface if men are to stand on it. In the later stages of building the new Bowhill cross-wall, where the material was shuttered, the masons introduced a raised spine of cob centrally along the top of each course, arguing that this provided some mechanical keying for the succeeding course. No other special arrangements were made at Bowhill; each course was simply built up on the one below when the latter was judged stable enough to accept it without deforming.

Course drying time has been discussed above, the situation at Bowhill not being typical because of the particular staff management arrangements at the site. However, there was one aspect of the cross-wall works, related to drying out, which was peculiar to the building. The wall was within the shell of the house, protected from the rain and sun, but also from the wind. In certain conditions wind helps to speed evaporation at the damp wall-face and is thus a factor influencing drying-out time in cob. That it was not a major part of the equation at Bowhill certainly means that drying time was slowed. As the works carried on over the winter the matter of humidifiers was raised but advice from the Building Research Establishment was that money might be spent, and little gained, by their use. So the wall was left to dry in its own time with no artificial aids. There may be advantages in a lengthy drying-out period. Speaking from experience, Alfred Howard maintains that the strongest wall in a cob building is always that facing most nearly north. His view is that the heat of the sun on a newly built, wet, wall produces, through speedier drying, a less homogenous result than where the wall is shaded.

At Bowhill, each course was, in the traditional way, constructed with a roughly regularized overhang to each side. As noted earlier this extra margin of material allows for exact trimming, or paring, back of the wall's face at

Figure 76 Paring: (a) mattock in use at Bowhill; (b) rick-knife known to have been formerly used in paring (brought to Bowhill by Mike Perrett); (c) sketch, not to scale, of nineteenth-century plasterer's 'salve'; (d) cob-parer, drawn to scale, as described by Clough Williams-Ellis 1919–20; (e) slasher and mattock used at Trusham, 1992, for cob-paring.

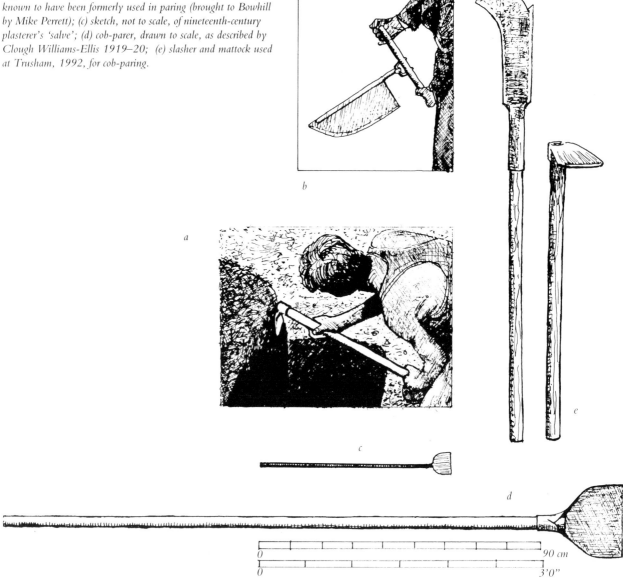

Figure 77 left, adze in use for paring, Bowhill, 1991; right, hacking-back with mattocks, Down St Mary. The frame on the left forms a temporary shutter to the end of the wall. (Copyright: Ray Harrison).

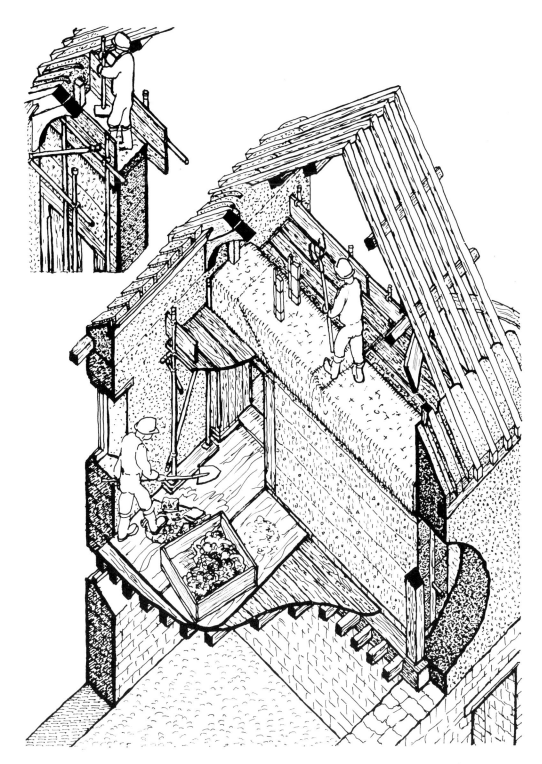

Figure 78 Bowhill, diagrammatic sketch of the cob cross-wall: building the cob wall and beam-filling: shuttering arrangements (top left).

a later date. Once each course has gone off a little (and sometimes sooner), it is pared back square. Its top arrisses then form the guidelines to which the course above is laid, overhanging as before. At Bowhill, in the lower part of the wall, two courses at a time were pared together, possible because the work was done over the autumn with the material drying out only slowly. It was found that to succeed fully with paring, account had to be taken of the Bowhill cob's propensity to shrink inward as well as downward. What turned out to be over-enthusiastic paring back at the outset produced an end result where

continuing inward shrinkage finally brought the pared wall face a little behind its intended line. The cob used to build the lower part of the new cross-wall was, it must be said, relatively strong (clay-rich), and this of course exacerbated the situation. By the time the upper wall courses were being built, 15% sand was being batched into the raw material and shrinkage was thus reduced.

Many tools have been used for paring. Mattocks seem popular today but spades, hay knives, axes and the cob-fork itself were used in the past (see Fig 76). Clough Williams-Ellis's 'baker's peel' parer was probably part of nineteenth-century plasterer's equipment, and known as a salve. [34] At Bowhill the masons purloined a carpenter's short-handled adze for the purpose; Alfred Howard's workers preferred mattocks (see Fig 77).

The fifth course of cob brought the wall level with the top of the timber lintels of the door frame. Matters were arranged so that this was much shallower than the rest, thus its downward shrinkage would be much less than that of its predecessors. Assuming the courses below underwent their major downward contraction before the fifth course was laid, it was felt that this thin levelling bed would quite quickly provide a stable base for the sixth course. The latter had now to extend continuously over the door lintels. In practice, and in combination with the slip-plane described earlier, this strategy seems to have worked for, as noted before, there was (to date) minimal fracturing of the wall at the door-frame corner. The sixth course of cob, extending the full width of the building, was the last to be laid entirely free (see Fig 78); from this point on shuttering was tried, again with the intention of further establishing the nature and performance of the material.

Shuttering the cross-wall

There are a number of nineteenth-century and later references to the shuttering of cob. A set of shutters of the classic rising variety, known to vernacular societies all around the world, was made in the late 1980s by John Vicary for use in cob-wall repair on the National Trust's estate at Killerton, near Exeter. [35] Charles Smith, mason and, latterly, Bowhill's site agent, considers that shuttering can be an advantage with wet mixes. In his view, free-build is quicker overall if a dryer mix is used; there is also, of course, less shrinkage with dryer material.

At Bowhill the first 'boxing' was made up of sheets of shuttering-ply fixed to, and reinforced by, softwood

Figure 80 Heavier-duty scaffold-board shutters, Bowhill 1992.

timber battens. The whole was supported by the existing scaffold on each side of the new wall (Fig 79). (Modern safety requirements meant that there had to be a permanent working platform at this level.) A seventh course was satisfactorily placed within this box, or trough, but the latter was really too flimsy for the pounding it had to take when the cob was being placed. The cob mix and laying methods were the same, essentially, as those already employed. The main difference was that heavy ramming of the soft material was technically possible, and a large paving maul was pressed into service for this. The shutters were struck after 24 hours.

For the eighth and ninth courses, the scaffold was adjusted for heavier, more robust, shutters (Fig 80). The original wall had tapered on one side. Shuttering formed

Figure 79 Frank Lawrence ramming cob in lightweight shuttering, Bowhill 1992.

Figure 81 Marks of boards, timber grain and shutter fixing-clips in cob, after striking shutters. Fibre lies in all directions, Bowhill 1992.

Figure 82 (above) Cob to the rafters, the cross-wall, Tom Perring on the top, Bowhill 1992.

Figure 83 (above right) Cob cross-wall: cob built out over the rafters, Frank Lawrence laying material, Bowhill 1992.

Figure 84 (right) Cob beam-filling to the cross-wall apex over cob and cob-blocks to the apex and also making good over original damaged cob beam-filling, all pared back level on completion, 1992.

from scaffold boards was constructed on the 'square' side of the wall only and the opposite, tapered, side was left open. A section of the jointed-cruck truss against which the wall lay acted as permanent one-sided shuttering at collar level, above the top lift of the scaffold-board shutters (Fig 80).

When cob is 'free built' the downward action of paring back causes fibre ends at the wall face to be exposed and bent downwards at the passage of the tool (see Fig 77). These ends usually drop away eventually but can sometimes be seen to survive in walling in protected places such as roof spaces, where the wall has never been plastered. On the other hand, where cob has been shuttered the fibre lies in all directions at the wall face (Fig 81).

The removal from each roof slope of those two rafters lying above the line of the wall facilitated the building of its upper section, allowing clear working space on the wall head as it rose (Fig 82). Once the wall's cob section

was raking-up level with the underside of the rafters, the missing rafter pairs were refixed. More cob was then beaten in between and over them to give maximum control of the drying process (Fig 83). Once gone-off, this 'permanently shuttered' beam-filling was pared back level with the rafter tops. The wall was then structurally complete (Fig 84).

Cob-blocks to the apex of the cross-wall

The decision to use cob-blocks at the apex arose from the Inspector's wish to complete the wall holistically in earthen materials, and from evidence of the original wall design. The cob, while set behind the abutting jointed-cruck truss as far as collar level had, above the collar, originally extended through the timber work to line with the truss's other face. The evidence for this was in heavy deposits of orange cob-dust on the underside of the jointed-cruck blades here. (The original builders must

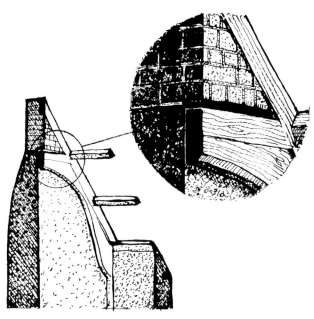

Figure 85 General part-section through cob cross-wall with detail of junction between cob-block apex and collar, showing gap between top of collar and underside of lowest course of blocks.

Figure 86 Tom Perring laying cob-blocks at the cross-wall apex. Note the appearance of the pared, unshuttered cob below the blocks and compare this with the effect of shuttered cob (see Figure 81), 1992. The peak of a gable is difficult to build and compress down in cob; it is more easily done in blocks.

have managed this without a problem. As we saw in Chapter 3, the clay content in their soil may have been very low.) It was feared that mass-cob built through to fill the apex triangle would fracture as it contracted down against the collar in drying. Cob-blocks made from the same material as the new cob were cantilevered into the truss apex from the top of the last course of mass-work which was finished a little 'proud' of the top of the collar. This left a gap between the top of the collar and the underside of the lowest course of blocks, allowing some downward shrinkage in the main wall (upon which the blocks rested) to take place without damage to the wall

(Fig 85). In the event, the arrangement appeared to work and there was no failure. The blocks were laid in a mud-mortar made from raw sub-soil from which all large stones had been sieved (Fig 86). For further details on block laying see Chapter 5.

PERFORMANCE

In all, the cross-wall took about 60 weeks to build, far longer than technically necessary, with the cob section complete in about a year. The completed works are shown in Figure 87. The later stages of the work were very protracted with staff away from the job for long periods, working elsewhere. The first four courses, to 6 feet (1.8m) high, were put up at a time when, tradition-ally, building in cob was normally avoided, ie between September and December 1991 in about 15 weeks, an average of $3^3/_4$ weeks per 1' 6" (0.45m) high by 30" (0.76m) wide course. Work at this time of year was, of course, only possible because the site was fully protected from the weather. At this early stage it actually took two men five days to prepare the cob and lay each course. This production rate was, it must be noted, considerably bettered at some other contemporary sites in Devon where work took place at a more appropriate time of year, where mechanization was greater, and where staff had considerably more experience at the outset than did the Bowhill masons. After 23 weeks or about 6 months, towards the end of the winter, downward shrinkage on this first section was 1" (25mm) overall. Linear shrinkage over the main lower section of wall from the new door frame to the north wall, some 11'3" (3.42m) was then between $1/_2$" (12mm) and $3/_4$" (18mm) overall, ie $1/_4$" (6mm) to $3/_8$" (9mm) at each end. After a further six weeks (early April 1992, as the weather became warmer) total linear shrinkage had risen to 1" (25mm) overall. When the wall had, as far as could be judged, undergone

Figure 87 Cob cross-wall complete and superficially dried-out. This side batters inward below the cob-block apex-panel, following the original arrangement, 1992.

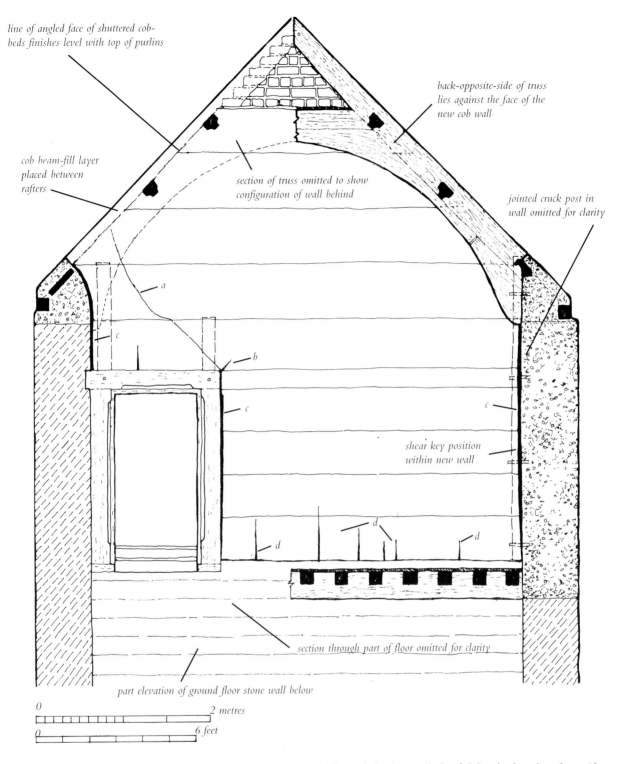

line of angled face of shuttered cob-beds finishes level with top of purlins

cob beam-fill layer placed between rafters

section of truss omitted to show configuration of wall behind

back-opposite-side of truss lies against the face of the new cob wall

jointed cruck post in wall omitted for clarity

shear key position within new wall

section through part of floor omitted for clarity

part elevation of ground floor stone wall below

a

b

c

c

c

d

d

d

0   *2 metres*

0   *6 feet*

Figure 88 The completed cross-wall: performance; (a) slip-plane, (b) incipient differential shrinkage-crack that failed to develop, showed one side only, (c) vertical shrinkage gaps away from fixed abutments, (d) short, variable-length vertical lines are stress cracks of a minor, non-damaging nature caused by friction between the main bulk of the wall, which attempts to shrink horizontally together as one mass, and the fixed masonry wall below. Generally, the extent of shrinkage here might have been further reduced by extra additions of sand. Given the wall's internal location this would have been quite safe.

of its shrinkage, some 16 months from its commencement, total linear shrinkage had increased to 2 $^3/_8$", or 1 $^3/_{16}$" (60mm, or 30mm at each end). Hair-line cracking in new plaster against the door frame showed that very minor movement was still going on a year later. Probably because of the long drawn-out later stages of building, the

fact that this was done in spring and summer and the addition of sand to the later mix, evidence of downward shrinkage in the upper wall courses after completion was negligible. The final pattern of shrinkage, showing in the face of the wall, is recorded in Figure 88, as is the arrangement of the courses.

5 Cob repairs

Good cob, a good hat and shoes and a good heart last for ever.

A Devon variation on the well-known theme

LOSS OF ORIGINAL FABRIC AND BEAMFILLING

Damage to the original cob and daub walling at Bowhill can be grouped under four main heads: that arising from inherent defects, damage from uncertain causes, damage due to failures of maintenance and general carelessness and deliberate damage resulting from alterations to and removals of fabric. By far the largest number of significant items of damage had been deliberate. The next largest group were maintenance failures, followed by those of uncertain cause. Two were likely to have been inherent defects. But the type of damage having the greatest impact on the overall structure seems to have arisen from maintenance failure. This must account for the major loss of the building's cob gables, and possibly for the loss of the north section of the West Range also. This balance between types of failure underscores the often quoted commonplace that with earth, maintenance must be consistently and thoroughly applied.

Some defects required little attention. This was the case with certain 'inherent' failures in the cob, for instance with the South Range, first floor, north elevation cob walling. Here fine vertical cracks through the wall coincided with jointed cruck positions. These cracks appeared to be the result of 'block' drying contraction where the wall thins down to receive jointed cruck-posts in vertical recesses. The fact that the recesses – chases – for the posts were cut after completion of the cob does not alter this diagnosis. [36] Experience at Bowhill suggests that after quite quickly undergoing its main shrinkage some material may continue to contract fractionally, as it dries for a while after it is put in position, with the chance of failure at any time during this period.

Other defects needing attention were dealt with relatively simply, perhaps by ramming-in small amounts of material, while others such as the preservation of an isolated remnant of cob in the east wall of the Kitchen, required very careful planning and execution.

Sometimes quite different, new, construction methods took the place of like-for-like repairs or reconstruction of original cob as in the case of the cob-blocks used at the top of the new cross-wall. The largest example of the use of alternative materials and methods for reconstruction was the west gable of the South Range (Figs 89 and 90). Here, for the original, lost, cob was substituted plastered and

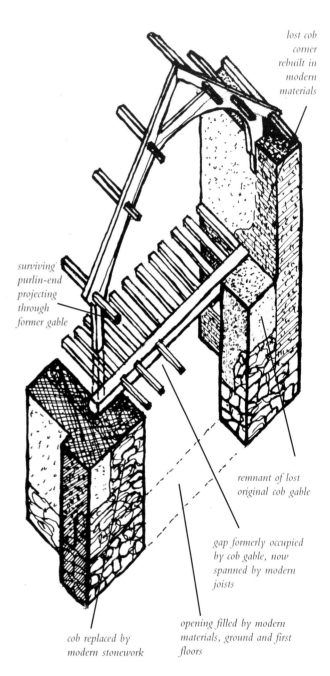

Figure 89 West gable: evidence for and analysis of former cob gable wall: cob dust at truss apex; purlins extend over gable-wall bay as extended tenons; surviving gable rafter shown in Figure 90; cob pier survives at ground floor; original stone wall base survives; modern inserted, short, joist-lengths span space where gable wall once was, to reach a thin modern external wall (omitted for clarity). (Drawing based on the record by Exeter Archaeology)

Figure 90 The west gable: photo shows half-purlins projecting past the end of the most westerly truss in the South Range, confirming the former existence of a thick gable wall, now lost, 1992. Figure 89 shows the main surviving features confirming that the gable had existed and that it was built of cob.

slate-hung timber framing. This expedient was adopted to help move the job to quicker completion than would have been possible had cob been used. Where possible, in the case-study reviews that follow, similar details of and reasons for the failures treated, will be given.

Beam-filling: general reinstatement

It is likely that an understanding of the value of cob as wall-topping and beam-filling [37] over masonry is as old in the region as the use of bedded stone itself. Alfred Howard may be expressing a wider local view when he notes that a substantial bed of cob over stone (a common feature in the west) will tie-in the top of masonry, though one might suspect post-rationalization in the knowledge that the modern reinforced concrete ring beam can indeed perform this function. Both stone and cob walls in the region can often be seen to have been raised at a later date by the addition of extra courses of cob on top of the original work.

The section of right-angled triangle at the wall-head, formed by the junction of rafter and wall, is an area for infilling, or beam-filling, to the angled top of which

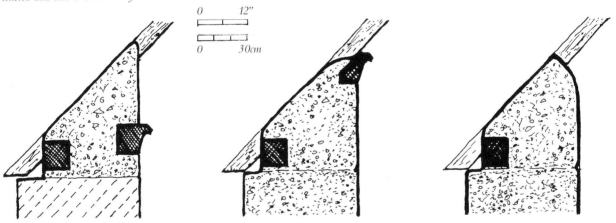

Figure 91 Sketches of three wall-head configurations at Bowhill. The two left-hand solutions might be described as 'high status' expensive details, the right-hand as 'vernacular' and economical. The 'rolled-in' cob wall head is seen in humble cob buildings in many parts of Britain.

Figure 92 Rubble beam-fill, Leigh Barton, Churchstow, near Kingsbridge, Devon, 1978.

Figure 93 New cob beam-filling over stone, compressed by foot and stick, between rafters, 1990. South Range, south wall. (Copyright: Ray Harrison)

rafters may relate or through or within which they may bed onto a real, or notional, flat wall top below. At Bowhill the rafters lie within the top of this infill but are actually supported, not on the wall-top but on eaves-purlins, free of the mass-wall (Fig 91). The term 'eaves-purlin' is used here in contradistinction to the term 'wall plate' in mass-walled buildings; the latter is always bedded directly on the wall-top. The eaves purlins are in turn supported at 'points', by the jointed cruck principals.

Cob offers a substantial solution to the problem of beam-filling. When done in stone, beam-filling could sometimes be more *ad hoc* and less workmanlike than in cob. Figure 92, showing rubble-stone beam-fill in a late medieval roof at Leigh Barton in Devon graphically illustrates this point.[38]

There has always been uncertainty about the place of shuttering in West Country tradition. Beam-fill between pairs of heavy rafters such as those at Bowhill must always have offered a practical example of the efficacy of the

method. The act of punning the material down from above with say, the squared end of a stick, is in these circumstances a natural and automatic technical progression, as the staff at Bowhill demonstrated (Fig 93).

Cob beam-filling in the South Range occurred originally above the stone, as well as cob, walling and was all reinstated. It had suffered degradation everywhere (Fig 94), partly due to the ingress of water in small amounts over long periods of time and partly no doubt due to damage done during the at least two full re-roofings given to the building in its 500-year life. There are three differing eaves-purlin details at Bowhill (see Fig 91), the principle of reinstatement of beam-fill being the same in each case. The degree of general erosion allowed new cob placing to be continuous, this being accomplished with complete success. No cutting away below took place, the new being built directly off the weathered surfaces of the old. The relatively fine-grained locally derived cob used allowed a very sharp internal top arris

Figure 94 Eroded original cob beam-fill over cob. Note the rafter trenches, the rafters removed for repair, 1992. South Range, south wall.

Figure 95 Completed, repaired cob beam-fill over stone, 1990. South Range, south wall.

Figure 104 (above) Reinstatement 1: building up cob under the eaves-purlin, over the window embrasure. Tom Perring holds a cob-mallet, 1991.

Figure 105 (above right) Reinstatement 1: Frank Lawrence paring back below the eaves-purlin, 1991.

Figure 106 (right) Reinstatement 1: completed reinstatement including beam-filling to eaves, above cornice-plate, 1991.

grout into it from the side until it was apparently completely full.

The grout had two purposes; to form a sound bed, filling the voids within the diagonal fracture, and to lock the pegs securely into position. It was not expected to have any glueing effect. For syringing (using veterinary syringes as for historic plaster consolidation), grout was made up of liquid lime putty, HTI powder, acrylic emulsion and sodium gluconate. (For details of the mix and process see endnote 43.)

The reinstatement of the wall-head could now commence. The first course extended half way up to the underside of the outer eaves-purlin and was about 12" high (300mm). It was impossible to get on top of the wall here. The material was therefore beaten-in heavily from outside and inside at the same time (see Fig 104). The succeeding courses followed and were eventually rammed close up under the outer purlin. Work then had to cease

as the inside face began to belly under the pressure of blows to the outside. In due course, another bed was added, beating by mallet and stick, as before. This course was in turn stopped, quite close up under the eaves (cornice) purlin inside. This was so that the final, shallow, course would undergo only minimal downward shrinkage when eventually placed and gone off. As can be seen from the illustrations, this strategy worked well. Paring is shown in Figure 105. When downward shrinkage had apparently ceased the upper section of beam-fill was added over the eaves purlin, finishing between each rafter in a sharp arris of cob (Fig 106).

The key lesson learnt here was that with careful planning and workmanship cob can be beaten into spaces below obstructions, in this case eaves-purlins, to a level where shrinkage is minimized. The before-and-after record is shown in Figure 107. Final shrinkage under the eaves (cornice) plate is shown in Figure 27.

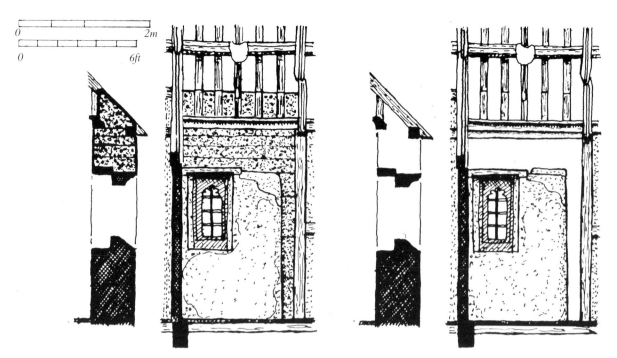

Figure 107 Reinstatement 1: condition before (right) and after (left) the works. (After Exeter Archaeology)

Reinstatement 2: rebuilding cob within a redundant flue (Inner Chamber)

In the corner of the first floor Inner Chamber in the south range a chimney-flue had been inserted in the cob wall thickness in the eighteenth or nineteenth century (Figs 108 and 109). This void was to be filled, building on the successful approach to the first reinstatement (Fig 110). The flue, set within the thickness of the wall, was to be capped low down and filled in with cob above in a series of small lifts. The courses were to be kept low to reduce the danger of unequal vertical shrinkage against the existing, abutting, cob. The latter was to be trimmed as necessary to effect a sound junction with the new work. The requisition noted:

> Cut back (absolute minimum) at exterior wall faces for level beds between old and new. Thoroughly mist-spray all existing cob that will be in contact with new work until water runs. Ensure old cob stays wet throughout the operation. (Architect's Requisition, 6th March 1991).

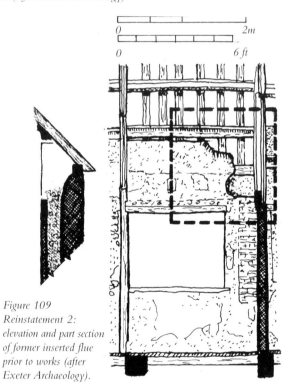

Figure 109 Reinstatement 2: elevation and part section of former inserted flue prior to works (after Exeter Archaeology).

Figure 108 Reinstatement 2: location diagram: South Range, first floor north-east corner of Inner Chamber.

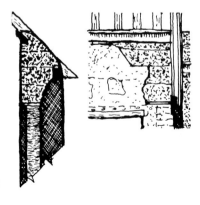

Figure 110 Reinstatement 2: part-elevation and part section of reinstatement of walling within later flue. (after Exeter Archaeology)

Figure 111 Reinstatement 2: flue condition prior to work, after capping flue in slate, 1991.

Figure 112 Reinstatement 2: Frank Lawrence cutting out level beds adjacent to flue, 1991.

Figure 113 (above) Reinstatement 2: spraying-up for new cob, 1991.

Figure 114 (right) Reinstatement 2: completed repair, former flue to right-hand of photo, 1991.

It is important that existing cob be kept wet where new work is being placed up to it. No difficulty was found in doing this using light, hand-operated mist-spraying to control surface scouring and erosion (see Fig 113).

The flue at low level was cleaned out and filled with pulverized, dry sieved, cob. (There was no danger of damp entering it.) Where it was exposed low in the wall it was capped with two thicknesses of slate with the edges chased into the surrounding cob using a mason's scutch-hammer and trowel-edge (Fig 111). Existing degraded cob to the side of the flue was cut back to sound material as required, without any problem, using a saw (Fig 112).

The cutting back of historic fabric is always a contentious matter. With hindsight it might have been possible here to build out the degraded cob-faces to produce the sound junction required. This could, however, have involved the introduction of lime in one form or another, or the treatment of the inadequate junction between old and new as a face-repair later. In the event, the method

chosen worked satisfactorily. (For details of lime/cob mixes see below.)

As this repair work started at the end of April (the start of the appropriate season for working with cob) a brief note on setting-time is relevant. The first course, some 9" (225mm) deep by 12" (300mm) wide, went off sufficiently, in a week, for the next course to follow on then. Five courses of varying thicknesses were placed. The upper two ran right through the wall. Again there was no chance of treading the material down and it was all hammered into place with mallets and stick-ends. Following completion of the main reinstatement, new beam-filling was carried on above in the usual way. Final downward shrinkage was minimal, the result of 'thin-bed' work with allowance for reasonable drying/setting periods between each course. By plugging a void the completed job brought the abutting jointed-cruck post back into the structural stabilizing system provided by the building's mass-walls (see Figs 110 and 114).

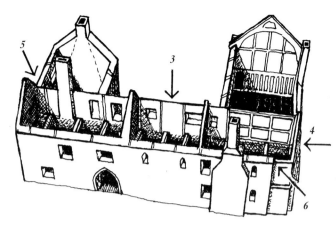

Figure 115 Reinstatements 3, 4, 5 and 6: location diagram.

Reinstatement 3: half- and full-depth wall repairs (Inner Chamber)

On completion of the works to the former flue two more adjacent areas of damage were tackled, using the same basic approaches (Fig 115). One involved full 'through the wall' reinstatement to make good an area of recent damage where pipework had been carried to the outside through the cob, leaving a large awkwardly shaped hole. No cutting-out of existing material was needed here. Before and after views are seen in Figure 116 (before) and Figure 117 (after).

The second case involved what might be called 'intermediate-depth' wall-face repair to internally eroded cob on each side of a jointed-cruck post in the wall (Fig 118). Because these cavities were quite large-scale and

Figure 116 (left) Reinstatement 3: effect of damage by former pipework flue carried through the wall, prior to works, 1991.

Figure 117 (above) Reinstatement 3: detail of completed reinstatement to former flue-hole, 1992.

Figure 118 Reinstatement 3: intermediate-depth damage prior to works, 1991.

Figure 119 Reinstatement 3: scutched-back, repaired intermediate-depth damage, 1992.

already relatively deep, it proved possible, again without any cutting out or back, to build them out using a series of rammed beds, as before. Ramming was by short, square-ended lengths of 1½" x 1½" (38 x 38mm) timber. The background was wetted up as before. No arrangements for tieing back the new work to the existing cob behind were made, nor were the edges of the original depressions cut back to master the new work.

Figure 119 shows the intermediate-depth re-instatement after paring back. The marks of the teeth of the scutch hammer are clearly visible. The work when initially complete stood proud of the general wall-face, for bringing into line later. Note the continuous indent at the junction of the old and new work. The technique of 'building out and over the existing', helps to avoid this small imperfection. Figure 120 shows both repairs completed.

Reinstatement 4: cob offset (Great Chamber)

During works to a small external high-level cob offset over stone at the south-east end of the Hall, parts of which were degraded, it was decided to experiment with cob- and cob-block reinstatement. Richard Baker's working drawings, reproduced here as Figure 121 (overleaf), show clearly the problem and its solutions. One end was rebuilt in cob in layers as for reinstate-

Figure 122 Reinstatement 4: Mike Perrett placing cob-blocks, 1992.

ment 2. During the placing of the upper course, a timber fixing-ground was built into the raking top to take a slate coping. This followed the original arrangement. An area of eroded face-cob to the right of this cob repair was then cut back slightly to take 4" (100mm) deep cob-blocks. The blocks were bedded in a slurried cob-mortar (the cob being sieved) to give an immediate permanent tight fit (Fig 122).

Reinstatement 5: pier-head repair (kitchen)

Part of the remnant of a cob pier-head in the south-west corner of the Kitchen, at the first floor, was almost detached from the surrounding fabric (Fig 123). The top was in a very fragile condition, having been eroded down from its junction with the inner and outer eaves-purlins. At high level its internal face carried a short but worrying

Figure 120 First floor cruck bay and cob wall associated with reinstatement 3 on completion of repairs, 1992.

Figure 123 Reinstatement 5: cob-pier, kitchen, before repair, seen from inside, 1993.

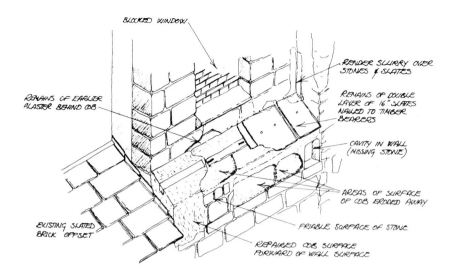

BLOCKED WINDOW

REMAINS OF EARLIER
PLASTER BEHIND COB

RENDER SLURRY OVER
STONES & SLATES

REMAINS OF DOUBLE
LAYER OF 16" SLATES
NAILED TO TIMBER
BEARERS

CAVITY IN WALL
(MISSING STONE)

AREAS OF SURFACE
OF COB ERODED AWAY

FRIABLE SURFACE OF STONE

EXISTING SLATED
BRICK OFFSET

REPAIRED COB SURFACE
FORWARD OF WALL SURFACE

DETAIL AS EXISTING

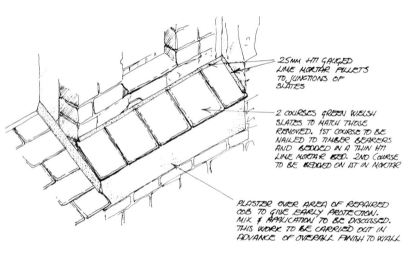

25MM HTI GAUGED
LIME MORTAR FILLETS
TO JUNCTIONS OF
SLATES

2 COURSES GREEN WELSH
SLATES TO MATCH THOSE
REMOVED. 1ST COURSE TO BE
NAILED TO TIMBER BEARERS
AND BEDDED IN A THIN HTI
LIME MORTAR BED. 2ND COURSE
TO BE BEDDED ON 1ST IN MORTAR

PLASTER OVER AREA OF REPAIRED
COB TO GIVE EARLY PROTECTION.
MIX & APPLICATION TO BE DISCUSSED.
THIS WORK TO BE CARRIED OUT IN
ADVANCE OF OVERALL FINISH TO WALL

COMPLETED WORKS

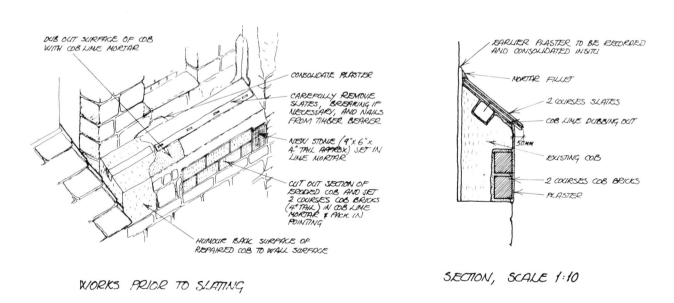

DUB OUT SURFACE OF COB
WITH COB LIME MORTAR

CONSOLIDATE PLASTER

CAREFULLY REMOVE
SLATES, BREAKING IF
NECESSARY, AND NAILS
FROM TIMBER BEARER

NEW STONE (9"x 6"x
4" TAIL APPROX) SET IN
LIME MORTAR

CUT OUT SECTION OF
ERODED COB AND SET
2 COURSES COB BRICKS
(4" TAIL) IN COB LIME
MORTAR & PACK IN
POINTING

HMMOUR BACK SURFACE OF
REPAIRED COB TO WALL SURFACE

WORKS PRIOR TO SLATING

EARLIER PLASTER TO BE RECORDED
AND CONSOLIDATED IN SITU

MORTAR FILLET

2 COURSES SLATES

COB LIME DUBBING OUT

50MM

EXISTING COB

2 COURSES COB BRICKS

PLASTER

SECTION, SCALE 1:10

Figure 121 Reinstatement 4: works requisition drawings, by supervising officer Richard Baker, 1992. (Copyright: English Heritage)

Plate 1 The east elevation of the Great Hall in 1993, stripped of its modern finishes. From left to right, the eastern doorway to the screens-passage, the chimney-stack flanked to each side by the hall windows and the north extension lean-to. Above the stone base the latter is a reconstruction from the 1980s. Composite construction is apparent in the contrast in colour and texture between cob and stone.

Plate 2 The interior of the Great hall on completion, looking south to the screens passage and double entrance to the Parlour. Beyond can be seen the Parlour fireplace. The floor, carried out under the first stage works, is of cob-lime. With a few exceptions new plaster and limewash obliterate variations in walling material to recreate something of the architectural effect intended by the builders. In this the display of roof structure plays a major part.

Plate 3 East elevation of the Great Hall and South Ranges in 1995, their composite construction lime/sand-rendered throughout and then limewashed, much as they would have been in 1500. Localised variation in wall plane surface remains considerable and areas of disturbance of the original fabric 'grin through' in places. These deliberately indicate former arrangements where now lost structure once abutted what survives. They confirm a reduction in size of the original concept. The set-back and smooth-rendered first floor gable to the end of the South Range carries the same 'archaeological' message of loss of earlier fabric.

Plate 4 The north, courtyard, elevation of the South Range in 1994, stripped of its damaging twentieth-century renders. Generally, in what survives, stone was preferred for load-bearing structures, cob functioning as a non-structural, 'enveloping', element. Stone fulfills this role here, supporting the first floor and cob-work above. In addition the internal cruck posts carrying the roof are mostly founded on the masonry, carrying their load down vertical chases in the cob. An important archaeological feature here is the horizontal scar and row of holes in the cob at about the level of the first floor window cills. This indicates the truss and common rafter system of the missing pentice. Combined with another scar of the Great Hall west wall this evidence enabled the roof slope, basic roof structure and extent of the pentice to be established, assisting in the design for its reintroduction.

Plate 5 A detail of a section of remaining c 1500 beam-filling to the wall head of the South Range, 1992; note the five-hundred-year old straw ends. The rafters have been removed for repair, depressions in the cob showing where their undersides lay. The scale in the foreground rests on top of the eaves purlin in which, on the left, can be seen the housing for a rafter 'birdsmouth'. Part of a windbrace intrudes on the right. The cob originally extended further upward and outward to overlie the eaves purlin as in the rebuilt section shown below. It has therefore been much degraded.

Plate 6 A section of South Range beam-filling restored to its original profile, covering the eaves purlin and with rafters in position, in 1990. On the far left original material awaits 'making up'. On the far right is the flank of the South Range chimney stack. Of interest here is the use of cob beam-fill over stone, and the 'flying' eaves purlin supported on the main trusses rather than on the masonry. In fact cob here has also been reinstated below the eaves purlin, on top of the stonework. The surface of the new cob shows regular horizontal striations produced by paring back the material which was initially built up proud of the tops of the rafters.

Plate 7 South-east corner of the Kitchen during repairs. The building's secondary constructional system, involving oak first floor timbers is shown. This is an inserted nineteenth-century first-floor structure using c 1500 first-floor timbers from another, demolished, part of the building. The timber lintel is original and spans what was probably a combined food hatch and door.

Plate 8 First floor window in the South Range, 1993. The timber inner lintel at the top of the photograph is original. Left of the lintel is a section of free-spanning cob extending to the rear of the (hidden) outer lintel, a typical Bowhill detail. In the face of the cob reveal nails have been temporarily inserted, their heads identifying the 'thin beds' of the cob construction used here.

New cob walling

Plate 9 Cob stockpiled on the scaffold below, for placing on the wall head, 1992. The translucent sheeting at the sides of the scaffold, with galvanised iron sheeting above, provides a protected working environment. On the purlin in the foreground are scratched carpenters' assembly marks.

Plate 10 Paring back new cob in the north wall of the Great Chamber, 1991. Visible in the background is the completed daubing to the partition between Hall and Great Chamber. A variety of timber repairs and reinstatements show in the roof structure.

Plate 11 The completed cob section of the new South Range cross-wall viewed from the Inner Chamber. The whole shows the effect of paring, including the top-most courses. The latter, though shuttered on this side, were still pared back. When the photograph was taken in 1992 the upper area had dried to a lesser extent than the work below, hence its darker colour.

Plate 12 Detail of the pared cob shown in Plate 11. The holes in the surface result from the dislodging of stones in the wall as paring goes on.

Plate 13 A small area of surviving original ceiling daub over the rafters at the junction between the South and Kitchen Ranges. The vertical striations on its surface show how it was smoothed down into place, perhaps using the edge of a board or something similar. The degree of drying shrinkage matches that which occurred when the ceiling over the Great Chamber was redaubed as part of the repair programme (see Plate 15).

Plate 14 Detail of surviving c 1500 double lath daub in the partition between the Hall and Great Chamber. Note the fibre and stone in the mix as well as the area of thin lime plaster.

Plate 15 'Fisting-on' ceiling daub in the Great Chamber, 1991. For details see Ceiling daub reinstatement. *A substantial repair to the base of a principal rafter can be seen below the purlin, to the right of the craftsman. The carved bosses masking the junction between truss and purlin are original features.*

Plate 16 Beating-in new daub in the Great Chamber / Great Hall partition, 1991. The new daub has been carefully carried around the remaining original material which shows as areas of lighter red. The lime grouting of the c 1500 daub has left a network of white lines in the cracks in its surface (see under Consolidating surviving original daub). *Larger white areas are original plaster. Beyond the workman is the top of the cob pier repaired under Reinstatement 1.*

Plate 19 A window reveal in the Inner Chamber, South Range. This was reinstated in heavily haired daub plaster, a historic secondary finish. The cob internal wall face here is finished in the more usual sand/lime mix. Where the two finishes meet, at the junction between reveal and internal wall face, the uneven substrate is expressed in a wavering vertical line. Such unevenness is now a characteristic of the overall aesthetic of the building, setting the experience of Bowhill's internal spaces far apart from that of any modern interior.

Plate 17 Applying thin lime plaster to wetted-up cob, the new cross-wall, 1993. Dubbing-out shows in the lower part of the wall

Plate 18 New limewashed plastering, the Great Chamber, 1995. The panel of original daub shown in Plate 16 is in the upper left panel of the framed wall on the left. It is provided with a hinged cover for protection and to allow viewing.

Figure 124 Reinstatement 5: cob-pier after repair; cob built up from the pier-head and then through and over the rafters, seen from outside, 1993.

fissure. By this stage, the confidence of the masons was such that the pier-head was reconstructed and its faces built up in cob alone. This was applied carefully, building out over the crumbling surfaces. The three rafters and inner and outer wall-purlins acted as shuttering, keeping the new work stable above as it was placed, locking the pier-head into place (Fig 124).

Reinstatement 6: cutting chases (Great Chamber)

The pier-head at the south-east corner of the South Range required reinstatement of missing beam-filling. Instead of ramming the new cob beneath and around the eaves-purlins and rafters, it was built up first as one mass. When this hardened, chases for one rafter and a flat support steel, to be placed into position subsequently, were then sawn into it, finished with the scutch hammer, as shown in Figure 125. This particular operation is an example of the flexibility in use of mass-cob where 'cutting out afterwards' can be a practical proposition.

Reinstatement 7: small-scale damage and failure, internal elevation (Inner Chamber)

Major reinstatement works 2 and 3 had already been done here, in bays 5 and 6 (Fig 126). It was decided to attempt to fill the remaining small wall-face cavities in bays 5, 6 and 7 with cob only (Fig 127, overleaf). A number of these cavities had been left by later, inserted ceiling joists, subsequently removed. The intention was to determine just how far working with cob mixes alone could be carried, with the qualification that briefly, at the outset, a dung admixture was tried.

The record does not suggest that dung was ever deliberately added to cob in the West Country. The issue was not explored at Bowhill other than this experiment with one small cob-repair section in bay 5 (although dung was added to crack filling mixes, see *Making good cracks in new daub, Great Hall*, below). The material had been stored for a while in plastic bags and was 'aged'. The results of its use in this form, mixed with cob, were inconclusive and its employment for this purpose was pursued no further, to the general relief of staff. It may be that dung needs to be fresh in order to perform satisfactorily in building works.

Filling of simple wall-face cavities was attempted in two ways; in small horizontal beds, and by filling completely in one operation. Cavities were first enlarged

Figure 125 Reinstatement 6: new cob beam-fill at eaves cut out to take rafter and steel strap, 1991.

Figure 126 Reinstatement 7: repair location, first floor, interior of north wall of Inner Chamber.

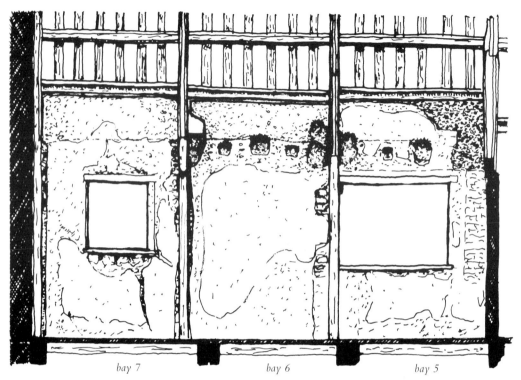

bay 7   bay 6   bay 5

*Figure 127
Reinstatement 7: Inner
Chamber, situation
before small-scale repairs
to cob walling. Damage
due to largely later,
inserted, beam sockets,
subsequently removed
(after Exeter
Archaeology).*

slightly internally to ensure that the cob was held in at some point (Fig 128a). Where beds were used these were allowed to go off in the usual way. Backgrounds were, of course, well wetted up (Fig 128b). The results here were quite satisfactory though external junctions with the original walling were indented slightly as described for reinstatement 3 (Fig 128f). However, even at this stage the masons had begun to extend their filling material out over the edges of the old cob (Figs 128d,e).

The second approach, filling in one, very quick, operation, was tried only once (Fig 129). As the mass dried out the patch edges, which had been feather-edged out over the existing cob, dried and lifted. The whole repair eventually shrank, dried and became loose (Fig 130). Clearly this particular cob could not be used to 'gob-up' holes quickly, as would be done with modern cementitious mixes, though some aftercare (see reinstatement 8 below) would have improved performance. Two related factors were at work here. Firstly the material had been placed 'instantly'. Secondly the mass had then simply been pummelled at the face, *in situ* in the hole. The mix may also have been damper than was strictly necessary. The main lessons learnt, and subsequently fully developed by the masons, were that for such continuous repair techniques to work, the material had to be as dry as possible and that it must be rammed at the stick end in very small amounts at a time, building out continuously and not placed in one mass. Even with these precautions, however, some aftercare is still likely to be required.

Works were also necessary in this area to the underside of two window sills and to a vertical fissure in the wall below one window (see Fig 127). The cill of one of these windows, of seventeenth-century date, was lifted to expose its fixing grounds. These were set in loose material, badly packed in. This might have been lime-grouted *in situ* but was decided to try to replace it with new cob into which the grounds were re-bedded. The cill was repaired and replaced. Window-height reveal boards at each reveal were inserted to give safe end bearings to the lintels above, since the opening was wider than originally, an example of SPAB-inspired 'honest propping'. The wall-face immediately below the cill was then made good by tamping in more cob. The second window was dealt with in much the same way. The wall-crack below the first window, which it had been thought might need lime grouting, was, on the engineer's advice, merely cleaned out at the surface to accept tamped cob surface-filling. It was not structurally dangerous (Fig 131).

Figure 131 Reinstatement 7: rammed cob filling below window-cill and to crack, 1992.

Figure 128 Reinstatement 7: (a) to (d) Inner Chamber interior of north wall: stages in filling redundant beam-end sockets using a sequence of small horizontal beds; (e) shows cob beaten-out over the edges of a hole after filling; (f) shows a repair pared back on drying, 1991 and 1992.

Figure 129 Reinstatement 7: hole filled at one go, rammed as one mass, 1991.

Figure 130 Reinstatement 7: detail of fill in Figure 129 on drying: edge peeling, 1991.

The last example under this head involved the filling of a length of redundant electrical conduit chase. Because this damage was quite shallow and square-edged in cross section, it was possible to fill it at one go, by ramming, working from one end to the other. No cutting out took place. Linear shrinkage produced a number of spaced out cracks in the dry repair exactly as with the test-box cob samples described earlier. These seemed not to affect the soundness of the work, which held in place well. This fact suggests that in this particular case, whatever minor bonding to the substrate behind occurred must have continued after the through-cracks had formed (as they imply movement of the material).

Reinstatement 8: further surface building-up works above the door between the Oriel and Kitchen Chambers

This reinstatement, though to a deeper indent than most, is typical of many others carried out to interior walls following the development by the Bowhill masons of their skills in handling the material (Fig 132). It included the 'cobbing-over' of a stainless steel plate set into the face of the wall at the upper-left of the door lintel (Fig 133). The new material was applied continuously. The works photograph clearly shows the overlapping patches of cob built up to produce the repair (Fig 134). They should be compared to the layers of daub in the illustrations of works to the inside of the Kitchen north wall below. The works sequence was as follows: brush off surface dust, well wet down, continue to keep old exposed cob wet throughout the operation, ram-in average stiffness new cob in small amounts at a time (Fig 134), lap the new over the repair edges, avoiding feathering out initially; come back and knock down edges as they peel on drying (aftercare). Figure 135 shows the damp completed repair.

Figure 133 Reinstatement 8: condition prior to works, stainless steel plate upper left, 1992.

Figure 134 Reinstatement 8: applying relatively stiff cob in layers, to build out wall-plane continuously. Mike Perret ramming in small hand-held amounts, 1992.

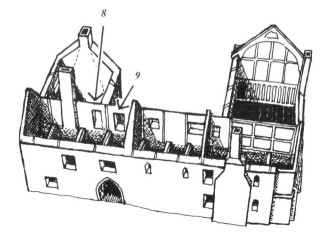

Figure 132 Reinstatements 8 & 9: repair location, areas above door lintels, north wall of Oriel Chamber.

Figure 135 Reinstatement 8: completed works; stainless steel plate concealed, upper left, 1992.

Reinstatement 9: 'hay daub' surface build-up above the door from Oriel chamber to former Gallery

In the early 1980s while researching the background to the tradition of the use of earth in the West Country, a description of daubing-out for repair of surface-damaged cob was given to the author. This involved building up the wall face in thin sequential layers of prepared hay daub, each having undergone 'initial set' before the next was added. The material was trowelled, and no doubt handed or palmed, on, and then also beaten back if necessary. It was decided to attempt this method in this location where the surface of the cob was generally eroded. The requisition recommended a pinned daub-mix (see below) but the mason chose to do the repair in daub alone. The earth used was sieved of stones above $^1/_2$" (12mm) diameter and mixed with chopped hay. The wall was well wetted in the usual way. The deepest, central section of eroded material was built out in two layers. The edges, curling as they dried, where overlapping the original cob, were dampened again and knocked back with a hard bristle brush. This treatment was applied everywhere, hence the slightly stippled appearance of the patch (Fig 136). Over the next few days it was necessary for the mason to come back to carry out this operation more than once, and also to spray and knock back a crack towards the centre of the repair.

Reinstatement 10: experiments with the pinning of repairs

For two trial areas in the Kitchen following this same basic technique, a daub-type mix was again made, using short, chopped, hay (Fig 137). The wall face was, as usual, first well wetted up. The daub, which was kept stiff, was in this case put on by trowel or hand in thin layers. It was found that in the small areas dealt with, a number of layers could be applied in a day. The record photographs illustrate the process better than any description (Figs 138 and 139). Note the difference in appearance between this and the previous repair, the one being trowel-finished, the other brush-stippled. To ensure that the earth patches stayed in place as they dried and to stop edges curling and thus to avoid aftercare they were pegged to their background with pins made from fragments of split deal. Often the heads of these pins were knocked over sideways into the daub.

Figure 136 Reinstatement 9: hay-daub build-up over first floor exterior door (Oriel Chamber), 1993.

Figure 137 Reinstatement 10: location sketch of pinned daub experiments, interior of east first floor wall and north gable, Kitchen

Figure 138 (right) Reinstatement 10: hay-daub applied using various placing methods, to level up damaged cob surfaces (Kitchen), 1992 (details of techniques scratched into repair surfaces).

Figure 139 (far right) Reinstatement 10: detail of layered hay-daub patches building out a shallow depression in cob (Kitchen), 1992. Edges pinned with deal slips.

Figure 140 *Remnant of daub-peg being withdrawn from part of the bee-infested cob section of Bowhill's south exterior wall, 1993.*

Figure 141 *Reinstatement 10 (continued): repair location: pre-pegged cob repairs in Oriel Chamber and below Oriel Chamber, to ground-floor stair-string chase in wall.*

a

b

c

d

Figure 142 *Reinstatement 10: (a) area for repair of window jamb, Oriel Chamber, cleaned out (brick is a nineteenth-century insertion), (b) small pegs hammered into cob; (c) reinstatement complete, still damp, and extended upwards as surface reconstruction; (d) completed, pared-back, repair showing slate packing between lintel and new cob below, 1993.*

The cob of the west end of the south elevation of the South Range harboured a long-established solitary-bee (mason-bee) colony. In the past, attempts to face it with pinned-daub had been made as it degraded from loss of render and bee-nest tunnelling action (Fig 140). The same condition was observed over the exterior of the remaining cob to the west wall of the Kitchen and in the return of the north boundary wall.

From wooden nails to hold daub in while it dries, it is a short step to the use of rather more substantial timber 'clouts' and pegs to keep full cob repairs set properly in position. For a damaged cob reveal to the former oriel window in the Oriel Chamber (Fig 141) a combination of small pre-fixed 'holding-in' pegs buried in, and steps cut into, the background cob was recommended. When it came to it, however, the slight toothing out or grooving of the background proposed in the works requisition was disregarded by the masons who preferred to clean out the

Figure 143 Reinstatement 10: Charles Smith starting to fill the stair-string chase working inward from the edges. Note the small pegs pre-set at varying angles, 1994.

failure and build directly from it (Fig 142a). Small pegs were hammered in (this is possible at the scale of peg shown) at varying angles and the new cob locked round these as it was laid, in three short lifts (Figs 142b and 142c). As the photograph shows, the new cob was built out and over the existing cob to help obviate edge lifting and indenting, as discussed earlier. When the initial set was past, the joint that had inevitably opened up between the underside of the lintel and the top of the new work was wedged, in the traditional way, with slate (Fig 142d). It should be noted that, in spite of its location, this remained a cosmetic, rather than a structural, repair.

The technique described above was adopted for the filling of quite a substantial wall-scar in the room below the Oriel Chamber. This had housed an inserted stair-string. Note that filling, which was here completed in one operation, takes place from the edge of the scar, working inwards in quite small amounts at a time. This ensures that the new material is very solidly compacted as work proceeds. It is essential, for the repair to succeed, that the new cob is everywhere brought into the closest mechanical association with the well-wetted surface of the old. Ramming in small packets at a time over the whole background helps to achieve this (Fig 143).

Though early experience at Bowhill had shown that horizontal obstructions within cob may impede downward shrinkage settlement, there was no external evidence of such damage from the small pegs used in the operations so far described.

The amount of aftercare called for at exposed repair edges where old and new join will vary and is dependent on the nature and consistency of the new material as well as the skill of the craftsman and the particular, localized, environmental conditions at the time the work is done, and then while it is drying. The speed of drying will obviously vary depending on time of year, degree of exposure to sun, whether or not there is a breeze etc. Over-quick drying out can be a hazard, as peeling of

patch edges results partly from (effectively unavoidable) variation in drying time between thicker and thinner areas of damp material. A traditional expedient of hanging wet sacking over the repairs, as employed with lime-renders, helping to prevent over-quick drying, was hardly used with the Bowhill cob repairs. It may well be worth considering, especially over external repairs taking place in strong sun. Even this approach, however, will involve a form of aftercare since the hessian must be regularly sprayed to keep it damp. In this case some attention was given later since, as drying proceeded, 'the edges peeled a bit'. The mason therefore went back, wetted the background and added more cob at the perimeter, beating-in the detaching sections at the same time.

The engineer subsequently recommended the use of heavier wooden pegs where beam-filling was to be reinstated over the door between the Oriel Chamber and the Kitchen (Fig 144). The intention was to mechanically

Figure 144 Reinstatement 10 (continued): repair location: wall-head cob reinstatement, South Range/Kitchen Chamber doorway.

Figure 145 Reinstatement 10: door between Oriel Chamber and kitchen chamber showing original cob beam-filling above with pegs for linking to new cob, 1992.

link a potentially unstable section of original cob, over a lintel that was to be replaced, to a reinstated section above and behind, which completed the lost beam-filling. Holes were pre-drilled in the original cob and pegs gently

tapped in (Figs 145 and 146). This was done without damage to the cob and it seems that again there was no sign of later shrinkage fracturing in the new work at peg lines. The lintel replacement referred to above is described later, under structural works.

Reinstatement 11: cob/lime mixes for reinstatement and repair

So far all the works described here have involved unadulterated clay cob. This section looks in more detail at repairs where lime and cob mixes were employed during the second-stage works at Bowhill. (Chapter 2 discusses the use of cob/lime during the Stage 1 works for the building and repair of the north extension to the Hall.)

The value of mixing lime with some earth materials has long been recognised,[39] powdered, hydrated, bag-lime being preferred by the workmen as easier to incorporate in the mix than lime putty. Alfred Howard demonstrated this approach, adding the lime to the mix before water, at one of his Bowhill training sessions (Fig 147).

The optimum ratio for the reaction of lime in cob has been shown to be between 3% and 10% by dry weight; there is apparently little advantage in adding more.[40] Generally, and as other works descriptions below will show, lime combines well with the red earths to produce

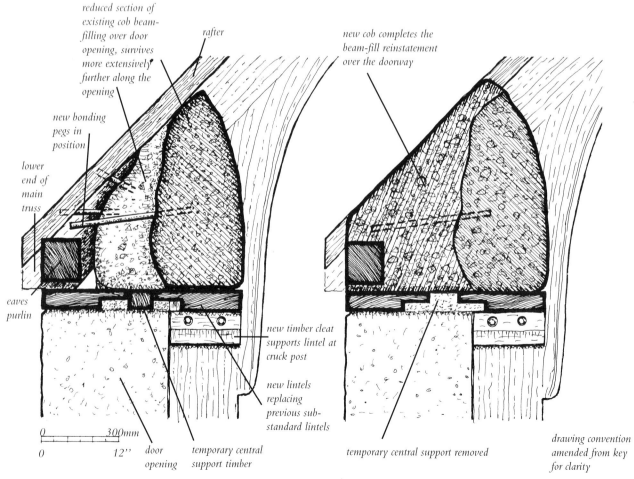

Figure 146 Reinstatement 10: diagrammatic sections through wall-head over Oriel Chamber/Kitchen Chamber doorway, pegs and new cob beam-fill. (Drawings based on A McCallum's specification drawing and completed works)

Figure 147 Alfred Howard treading-in bagged-lime, Bowhill training day, 1990. (Copyright: Ray Harrison)

Figure 148 Reinstatement 11: repair location: reveal of window in north wall, Great Chamber and interior of north gable, Kitchen.

very useful material, much liked by the masons, which hardens relatively quickly.

The working advantages of the combined mix are apparent from the photographic record of repairs and reinstatement to a window reveal in the Great Chamber (Fig 148). The material used was pre-prepared fibrous daub mixed in the ratio 2 parts daub to 1 of 'coarse stuff' (1:3 [lime:sand]). The area for treatment was partly rubble-stone and partly cob. It was brushed down and then sprayed in the usual way. The tactile, sticky nature of the cob/lime is very apparent from the illustrations (Figs 149a and 149b). It can be placed by hand (finished by trowel), as here, or, in the case of the heavier repairs, beaten in with tools (Fig 150). For built-out vertical-

surface applications, where the mix is very moist, as in Figure 149, there will be a limit to the thickness that can be applied at any one time, just as with conventional renders. Shrinkage-cracking was minimal with this particular repair and was controlled by trowelling back three or four times afterwards as the material dried.

On the Kitchen's north gable interior, water running down the side of the stone stack had, over long periods of time, probably brought about the extensive high level of weathering found in the cob abutting the flue. For the horizontally bedded cob-reinstatement to this interior face, the masons chose the composite material, adding 10% lime in hydrated form to the cob (see Fig 150). This was trodden dry into already fully prepared cob. It

a

b

Figure 149 Reinstatement 11: Great Chamber, (a) Tony Stoyles spraying up window reveal for cob/lime placing; (b) placing the plastic cob/lime mix, 1992.

Figure 150 Reinstatement 11: Kitchen gable, Mike Perrett beating in cob/lime against original cob, showing linking pegs, 1993.

Figure 151 Reinstatement 11: Works shown in Figure 150 as completed – cob/lime apex of cob panel, to left of stone, 1993.

produced a stiffer, less sticky and more cob-like mix than that made with putty-lime. In position the cob-lime arrived at an initial set more quickly, and with less shrinkage, than purely clay-bound cob. Compaction did not need to be so heavy, nor did the work take so long as with cob, being done in one staged but continuous lift in about a day and a half. The material went off quickly and was finished, as shown (Fig 151), to its intended final face-line and did not require paring back after setting, a saving in time, material and energy. (It should be remembered, however, that cob-lime is a denser material than pure cob. Ideal conservation practice seeks to 'mend' one material with another having as near as possible the same coefficient of expansion.)

Perhaps because of anxiety over the fact that cob-lime had less affinity with its cob background than has pure

cob, and because of the height of the area for repair, the masons introduced pegs to offer some mechanical connection between the two materials (see Fig 150). They cut back the foot of the eroded area a little to give a level bed and built up from this, pre-pegging vertically and horizontally as they went. If angled slightly upward into the new material, pegs projecting from the original cob could no doubt help to keep such a repair in place. Again there was no evidence of shrinkage failure on completion. As the photo-record makes clear, the finished appearance of the cob-lime at Bowhill was very different from that of the pure cob repairs. Stainless steel helical ties (see below) inserted when the repair was fully dry would be an efficient way of bonding old to new, perhaps allowing the new to function structurally to some extent.

Reinstatement 12: repairs and reinstatements using cob-blocks

Two cob-block reinstatements have already been described. One, external, was in the nature of an initial experiment. The other was an essential part of the cross-wall reconstruction. A further experiment was made. Apart from this, in the remaining cases described below, blocks were used either for convenience or because, as the job programme became tighter, it became impossible to allow for the drying out and settling period needed for cob works.

Cob-lime mortar was employed in one place only. This was on the advice of the author, at a time when there was concern about quick completion and it was thought that the addition of lime would improve speed of set and stiffen the joints to reduce shrinkage. Everywhere else, however, for mortar, the masons and site management used clay-based material alone, taking the view that lime in fact gave little advantage in terms of speed or joint performance.

Where blocks were relatively small, staff were content to use a sieved wet clay slurry with fines but no stones. For mortar for some of the work, damaged or discarded bits of cob-block waste were pulverized and the stones removed. This material, of course, contained straw fragments, already chopped in the case of Alfred Howard's blocks. On another occasion, again to stiffen the joint and perhaps with lime mortar technology in mind, the masons ground up brick dust and added this to their 'clay' mortar: a result of their frequent creative thinking. The dust will have helped to bulk out the joints. On yet another occasion, noticing that excavation in one of the ground floor rooms was producing stone-free sub-soil, they used this successfully for mortar (presumably this contained a reasonable proportion of sand).

Working on the classic principle that mortar in blockwork is there to take up irregularities between blocks rather than to glue them together, the masons found that with some small blocks they could rub down the mortar and block faces slightly as they built, to produce relatively thin joints. However, this was more difficult with the larger blocks which, because of suction, could not be easily moved about once placed. Mike

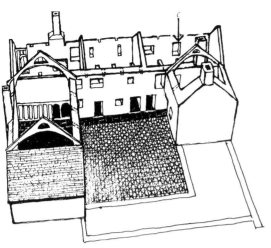

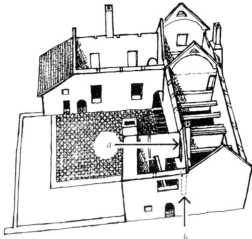

Figure 152
Reinstatement 12:
repair location, cob
block repairs; (a) new
cob-block pier to
doorway between
Oriel and Kitchen
chambers; (b) new
cob-block pier in
south-west corner of
Kitchen; (c) repair to
west reveal of (former)
oriel window, south
(interior) wall, Oriel
Chamber.

Perrett, the mason responsible for a major section of wall reinstatement in block, was unhappy with the resulting thick joints. He decided therefore to reinforce these by adding straw to his mix as for conventional cob. In this case joint drying shrinkage showed eventually as a minor horizontal crack at wall head. It should be noted that the block-work involved had only to support its own weight, over a storey or so. The results of load-testing the method could be of considerable interest.

In placing the blocks, conventional bricklaying practice was initially followed, ie blocks were dipped in water first before laying. Later, pre-spraying was preferred. There appear to have been no difficulties with this as the process does not involve saturation. The combination of wet block and wet mortar produced very strong initial suction making the bigger blocks, once placed, difficult to move, as described above. Larry Keefe found the suction to be so strong, during similar works at Bury Barton, that if removal of a newly placed block was attempted, the face remained behind, torn-off in the wall. As noted in Chapter 3, because of the method of manufacture, ie relatively stiff material rammed in moulds, blocks at Bowhill had to be face-bedded in the wall as for stonework. In other words they had to be laid on the same plane as that in which they had been moulded.

The remaining research-repair with cob-blocks tackled the right-hand internal reveal of the former oriel window, the Oriel Chamber (Fig 152). The failure, erosion back of the inner wall-face (for reasons unknown), in this case extended along the wall as far as the foot of a (truncated) jointed cruck post (Fig 153). The failed area was cut back in three steps and cob blocks were inserted, set in sieved mud mortar (Fig 154). The joint between the lintel underside and the top block was made up in slates packed in putty lime. The faces of the blocks were left proud of the wall face and were scutched back when the mortar had gone off. This repair is likely to prove structurally stronger than its pegged-cob partner opposite (Fig 155).

Cutting out and piecing in cob-blocks was also subsequently applied to a small area of degraded cob high up at the back of a niche adjoining the chimney stack in the Kitchen. Another reinstatement in cob-block related to

Figure 153 Reinstatement 12c: right-hand reveal of Oriel window (Oriel Chamber), fabric cleaned out before repair. The brickwork is nineteenth-century, 1993.

Figure 154 Reinstatement 12c: Charles Smith fitting cob-blocks to steps cut for repair. Note foot of upper cruck post above, 1993.

Figure 155 Reinstatement 12c: detail of completed cob-block repair with slate packing under lintel, 1993.

part of the dividing wall between the Oriel and Kitchen chambers, where a short missing section of external cob wall was rebuilt in block (Figs 152b, 156, 157 and 158).

A second reinstatement of missing cob wall was the formation of a new cob-block pier within the modern doorway between Oriel and Kitchen chambers (Figs 152a, 159 and 160). This brought the door reveal into line with the face of the Kitchen's abutting jointed cruck post, which had itself been missing and reinstated. The opportunity was also taken during this work to lower the

Figure 156 (top) Reinstatement 12b: new cob-block pier viewed from Oriel Chamber. Pier under construction, 1994.

Figure 157 (above) Reinstatement 12b: view of south-west corner of Kitchen with new cob-block pier built up to fill void to left of cruck post (centre), 1994.

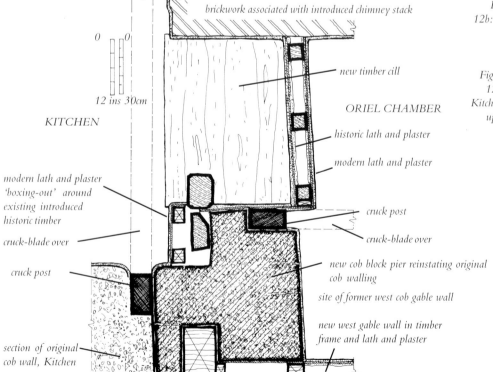

Figure 158 Reinstatement 12b: plan of new cob-block pier in between Oriel and Kitchen

door opening height to a level more appropriate to its context. This was the first section of cob-block to be given extra stability through the use of stainless steel helical ties, placed in joints and drilled into abutting timberwork to tie the structure together (Figs 161 and 162). As can be seen from the photo record the helical ties were driven in by mechanical hammer. An experiment with helical wall ties was carried out at Bowhill in February 1994 (see Table 4).

Table 4: Results of an experiment with helical wall ties, Bowhill

Location	Depth driven	Pull-out load
Historic cob (1)	5.5" (140mm)	2kN
Historic cob (2)	2.75" (70mm)	1.4kN
New cob (cross-wall)	4.4" (110mm)	2.5kN
Cob block (A Howard)	–	2.25kN

Figure 161 Stainless-steel helical ties. This type of wall-tie, driven in mechanically, is commonly used to anchor together existing fabrics (brick, concrete, timber) where repair is needed. It can be combined with grout to form a 'grout-anchor'. This was not necessary at Bowhill; the ties' corkscrew form appears very well adapted to use with cob. (Copyright: Helifix)

Figure 159 Reinstatement 12a: completed cob-block pier, south-east corner of Kitchen (doorway from Oriel to Kitchen chambers) visible to both sides of the cruck post (left), 1994.

Figure 162 Reinstatement 12a: drilling helical ties between courses of new cob blocks and into the side of the upper-cruck post, 1994.

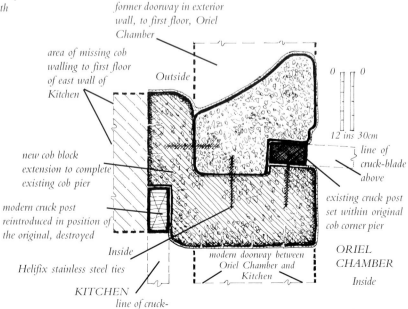

Figure 160 Reinstatement 12a: plan of cob-block reinstatement to south-east corner of Kitchen chamber. (Based on a drawing by D Evans)

former doorway in exterior wall, to first floor, Oriel Chamber

area of missing cob walling to first floor of east wall of Kitchen

Outside

new cob block extension to complete existing cob pier

modern cruck post reintroduced in position of the original, destroyed

Inside

Helifix stainless steel ties

KITCHEN

line of cruck-blade above

0   0

12 ins 30cm

line of cruck-blade above

existing cruck post set within original cob corner pier

modern doorway between Oriel Chamber and Kitchen

ORIEL CHAMBER

Inside

One tie was hand-driven in new cob to a depth of 90mm, when the pull-out load was 1.5kN. When removing the tie from the cross-wall it jammed and it was decided that this was probably because the core of the wall was still damp.

Reinstatement 13: blocking-up lost section of first floor external wall, east elevation of Kitchen

A storey-height first floor section of former external cob wall extending from the junction with the South Range to the jointed cruck in the east wall of the Kitchen was missing (Figs 163 and 164). The reasons behind the loss of this section of cob are complicated. It may have been damaged when the first floor was added to the Kitchen around 1800, when access to the abutting first-floor Oriel Chamber in the South Range could still have been by the original external first-floor gallery in the courtyard. Later the gallery with its external stair disappeared, to be replaced by an external diagonal passage at first floor, built out across the junction between West and South Ranges, from Oriel Chamber to the Kitchen. The whole area of cob wall in question may have been taken away at this time to facilitate the new arrangements. Because the roof at Bowhill is fully supported by the building's timber frame (jointed crucks and purlins) there was no structural disadvantage in doing this. Within the last 30 years, in the 1970s, this 'flying passage' (or bridge or bye-pass) was in its turn taken away and a doorway forced directly in the cob wall between Kitchen and Oriel Chambers. The now redundant wide opening in the upper wall of the Kitchen was not thereafter substantially closed. An element of lack of maintenance probably also contributed to this particular overall loss.

The photo-record shows the situation prior to the works with, outside, a modern felt sheet facing supported inside by light softwood studding (see Fig 164). Before reinstatement could begin a failed timber lintel below had to be made safe and some related fabric above it consolidated. This operation is discussed below in *Underpinning historic cob*, and is shown being completed in the progress photo (see Fig 187). Earth blocks were produced by Alfred Howard, chosen as a nominated supplier because of pressure of time.

During the planning of the work the idea of cavity-wall construction was raised. On a 24" (0.6m) thick wall this would save in numbers of blocks required and reduce loadings. The east-facing, sheltered aspect would mean that once rendered externally, rain penetration through the outer skin would be very unlikely. In the event the site engineer, Arthur McCullum, required diaphragm construction (Figs 165 and 166).[41] As before, the masons set stainless-steel helical ties into the mortar joints at the ends of the new work to help secure it to the existing structure. However, in this case, the ties were drilled into the face of the post and adjoining block-work at a slight angle. The interposition of the drill chuck above the block surface made angled insertion unavoidable (Fig 166). The masons considered this an advantage since the tie thus clipped the arris of the block where it lay against the adjoining structure, taking it from the putative joint into the fabric of the wall itself.

At its head the new wall was corbelled-in to lock continuously between the inner and outer eaves-purlins (see Fig 165). 'Scutching-back' or 'humouring-back' *in situ* earth blocks to a rounded profile of the sort required here is a very simple matter.

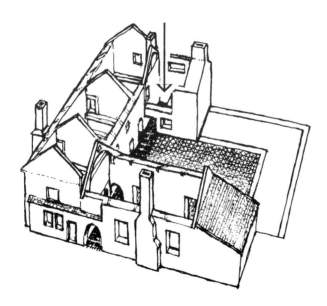

Figure 163 Reinstatement 13: repair location: first floor, Kitchen, east wall.

Figure 164 Reinstatement 13: external view of temporary panel closing area of missing cob first-floor wall, Kitchen, 1992.

Figure 165 Reinstatement 13: right, elevation of completed cob-block diaphragm wall, showing window-opening and lintel with former beam-end sockets to right of lintel (and below lowest course of new cob blocks) (after Exeter Archaeology); below, section through the new block wall: note lathing between lintels to window. (Based on a drawing by D Evans)

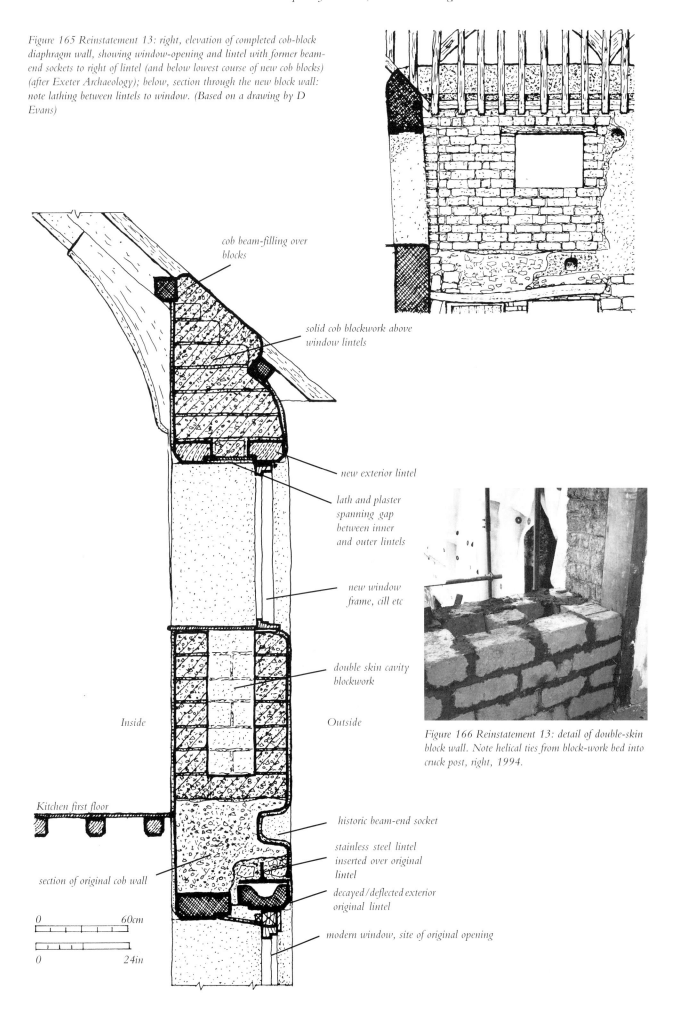

cob beam-filling over blocks

solid cob blockwork above window lintels

new exterior lintel

lath and plaster spanning gap between inner and outer lintels

new window frame, cill etc

double skin cavity blockwork

Inside

Outside

Kitchen first floor

section of original cob wall

historic beam-end socket

stainless steel lintel inserted over original lintel

decayed/deflected exterior original lintel

modern window, site of original opening

0   60cm

0   24in

Figure 166 Reinstatement 13: detail of double-skin block wall. Note helical ties from block-work bed into cruck post, right, 1994.

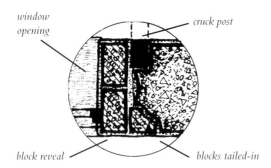

Figure 167 Reinstatement 13: plan-detail of junction management through tailing-in cob-blocks

Figure 168 Reinstatement 13: stabilizing original beam-socket hole with a fine cob mix, kitchen, 1994.

Figure 169 Reinstatement 13: completed double skin diaphragm cob-block wall, interior view, 1994.

At its south end the cavity work formed a continuous butt junction with the jointed cruck and the previously reinstated cob-block pillar. At the north end the irregular edge of the original wall had been pieced-in with modern brickwork. The brickwork was removed and was replaced by cob-brick 'tailed' into the existing (Fig 167). During this operation some of the adjoining, modern, cementitious render on expanded-metal lath stapled to the original cob, had to be cut away. [42] In removing the render, a socket for a former beam, possibly relating to the roof of the vanished outside gallery, was uncovered. It was one of a number of archaeologically significant holes up under the eaves. It had been somewhat altered by the previous application of stapled expanded metal lathing and cement render and its edges were carefully consolidated by hand-applying a soft cob mix (Fig 168). The interior of the completed blockwork is shown in Figure 169.

TIEING-BACK THROUGH COB

A common feature of the old tradition is the iron or timber restraining tie, usually across the width of the building and fixed to external timber anchor plates, to stabilize outward leaning walls. John Deal ARIBA, when speaking of the flexibility inherent in some cob, has described opposed gables as swaying about when a restraining rod between them was loosened (Figs 170a, 170b and 170c).

At Bowhill, two tie-rods fixed to a stainless-steel anchor-plate were threaded through the thickness of a wall to clamp a free end-section of eaves-purlin to its other side. The purlin in question, in the wall-head of the Oriel Chamber, abutting the Kitchen, was a reinstatement of an original length replaced by steel in the 1970s when a door between the two chambers had been made here (Figs 171, 172a, 172b and 173). All the beam-filling on the Kitchen side had been lost. This was subsequently replaced giving full stability in the completed arrangement.

STABILIZING WALL-HEADS AND REPLACING DOOR LINTELS

As noted above the opening between the Oriel and Kitchen Chambers had been made in the 1970s. It was decided to replace its lintels to improve detail (1970s steelwork, referred to above, had been involved) and to put back 'coherent' structure.

In mass walling, lintels are invariably set side by side across the wall thickness. In cob there are often quite wide gaps between them. To provide lintels for new openings in existing walls it is usual to cut a horizontal slot in one side of the wall, the width of one of the proposed lintels, and fit the latter to this, wedging and pinning above with slate or (as preferred by Alfred Howard), folding wedges as necessary. The process is then repeated for the other side and after this the opening can be cut away from below (Fig 174). Sometimes, trestle pieces in the form of 'needles' are passed through the wall thickness first, to

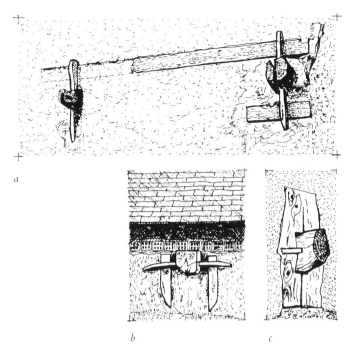

Figure 170 Traditional historic cross-tie end-securing methods for cob; (a) barn at Lower Woodbeare, Kennerleigh, mid-Devon (copyright: Ray Harrison); (b) house and barn at Montcuit, near St Sauveur Lendelin, Manche, Normandy (after a photo by Francis Kelly); (c) clay barn at Flatfield, parish of Errol, Perthshire (after Walker 1977, 58, fig 36).

a

b   c

Figure 171 Structural works, location of tieing-back repair, door between Oriel and Kitchen chambers, 1992.

a

b

Figure 172a (above) Structural works, tieing back through cob: horizontal stainless-steel plate set into cob and tied to new oak wall-head purlin on opposite side of wall by threaded bars, through wall thickness, 1992; 172b (above) opposite side of wall showing steel, subsequently replaced by oak, eaves purlin section.

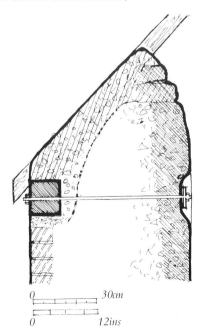

0 ———— 30cm

0 ———— 12ins

Figure 173 (left) Structural works, section through tieing-back arrangements shown in Figure 172.

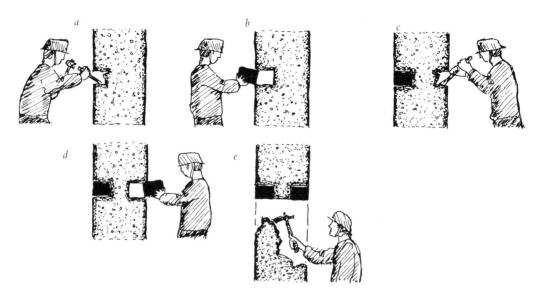

Figure 174 The principles of inserting a new opening into cob walling; (a) chase formed for one lintel; (b) lintel inserted on one side; (c) equivalent chase formed on opposite side; (d) second lintel in place; (e) cob cut away below lintels; opening formed.

each side of the head of the planned opening to ensure exact alignment of the lintels themselves as they are inserted. The process had already been carried out in poor softwood lintels to form this particular opening in the 1970s. New replacement oak lintels were therefore prepared, to the same depth as those existing.

Above the lintel on the Oriel Chamber side a substantial portion of original cob wall-head survived. On the Kitchen side its equivalent had completely disappeared. The site engineer was concerned that this remaining cob might also be lost during repairs. He therefore recommended the locking of the existing into newly placed cob behind (on the kitchen side). The reinstated cob would be on top of the section of new wall purlin, the latter replacing the steel shown in Fig 172b. The new cob was locked to the existing by means of the pre-placed internal dowels, a process described in Reinstatement 10 above (see Figs 145 and 146). Figure 175 illustrates the process of lintel-replacement associated with this operation. Figure 176 shows the underside of the completed works, with new cob above clear-spanning at the centre, between lintels.

REDIRECTING LOAD ABOVE FRACTURED COB

A doorway had been opened in the west wall of the Kitchen in the sixteenth century. Externally a segmental stone arch and jambs had been inserted into the opening (Fig 177 and see Fig 181). For more than half the depth of the wall (internally), the head to the opening was, however, unsupported cob, left as it had been cut. Cob is quite capable of spanning on its own in such situations, but the engineer was worried that in the particular circumstances it was overloaded.

Above and to one side of the opening (internally) an inserted main floor beam had subsequently been introduced, lowered down from above in a chase or 'pulley groove' pre-cut in the wall (this chase remained, filled with rubble stone) (Fig 180). It will be remembered that the Kitchen had originally been open to the rafters, the first floor being added c1800. Possibly as a result of floor load taken by the inserted beam, the unsupported cob over the door opening had fractured. A crack ran up at one side of the slightly arched cob-head towards the underside of the beam (Figs 178 and 179).

To relieve this failure of load it was decided to flitch and to hang the beam from above by means of stainless steel strapping up the wall, turned at cill level above, to spread the weight over a wider section of wall (Fig 181).

The photo-record shows the preparation for and the insertion of the flitch into the beam-centre (see Fig 180). This was resin-grouted in. The operation took advantage of the presence of the slot cut into the wall c1800 as a pulley groove to allow the sliding-in of the massive (re-used) floor-beam. As noted above, this pulley-groove slot had been back-filled with rubble. When it was cleaned of its rubble packing, the hearting of the beam-end was found to have rotted away. This was, therefore, reformed in resin as part of the flitching operation. Two vertical stainless steel rods, hangers, were bolted to a plate fixed to the flitch and were bolted again at top to a horizontal stainless-steel spreader-plate at window-cill level. The hangers were concealed within the old pulley groove (see Fig 181). The pulley-groove chase was then 'stoned-up' again to conceal the hangers, and the spreader-plate was 'lost' beneath window-cill 'make-up' and then plaster. The final result was a totally invisible mend. The crack in the cob was itself made good before plastering.

Figure 175 (far left) Structural works, door head between Kitchen and Oriel Chambers, one new lintel in place with second lintel being slid in from the opposite side by mason Mike Perret. Note the temporary central lintel propped from below on acro-props.

Figure 176 (left) Structural works, view of completed works from below. The temporary shutter support in the centre has been removed, leaving a section of new (reinstated) cob clear-spanning above, between the two new lintels, 1992–3.

Figure 177 Structural works, repair location diagram for redirection of load above fractured cob over doorway in ground floor Kitchen, west wall.

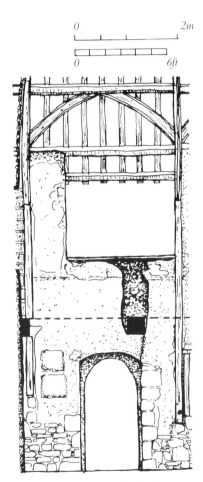

Figure 178 Works for redirection of load, doorway cut through internal cob with outer stone frame. Inserted stone facing to right. Crack in cob between top corner of later stone facing and underside of main beam, 1994.

Figure 180 Works for redirection of load, 'flitching' the main beam. Carpenter Martyn Clough fitting the stainless steel flitch-plate to the beam. Note the 'pulley-groove' in the wall, which originally allowed the beam to be inserted (probably early in the nineteenth century), 1994.

Figure 179 Area of works for redirection of load (after Exeter Archaeology).

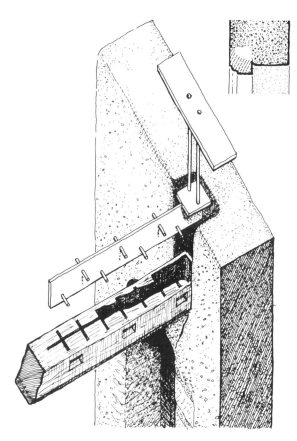

Figure 181 Works for redirection of load, diagrammatic view shows cob clear-spanning doorway with the hanger-and-spreader system removing the beam load from above the cracked section of cob. (Based on A McCallum's specification and completed works. Schematic only)

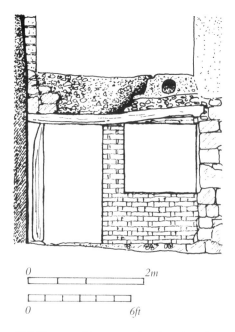

Figure 183 The area of the structural works, cob underpinning (after Exeter Archaeology).Existing prior to work.

Figure 184 Structural works, cob underpinning, the works area before commencement. Note decayed lintel, 1994.

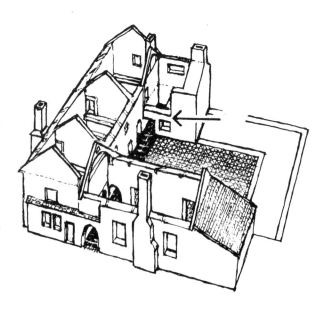

Figure 182 Structural works, repair location for underpinning historic cob, east wall exterior, Kitchen.

Figure 185 Structural works, cob underpinning, the cob socket filled with expanded polyeurethene and needled (ie metal bars passed through wall) below, 1994.

Figure 186 Structural works, cob underpinning, the cob and socket suspended in a padded cradle so that the later masonry below can be removed, one small section remains to be taken out, 1994.

Figure 187 Structural works, cob underpinning, the stainless-steel lintel is in place above the beam and below the cob in its padded cradle (right). Mike Perrett is building up the rubblestone underpin facing again, 1994.

Figure 188 Structural works, cob underpinning, the masonry is now completely rebuilt to support the cob. One or two needles remain to be withdrawn, 1994.

UNDERPINNING HISTORIC COB

This operation had to be carried out before cob wall Reinstatement 13 could be commenced. It involved works to a failed, timber ground-floor window-lintel and a section of wall resting on this, up to the level of the first floor, in the east elevation of the Kitchen (Fig 182). The wide double lintels here, spanning what was probably originally an external doorway and food-hatch combined, had deflected at some time and been supported towards their centre point by an inserted brick pier (see Plate 7). Within the wall the outer lintel was very badly decayed. Cob had originally been built up to form walling on top of the lintels; some low, surviving, sections were still of cob while other parts had been replaced in rubble stone (Figs 183 and 184).

A load-bearing stainless-steel T-section lintel was to be arranged, set above the failed outer lintel whose exaggerated deflection was historic (see Fig 165). The underside of the T-section was formed to follow the varying profile of the timber. Within the low section of surviving cob wall above the lintel was a substantial empty joist-socket related to the former gallery to the first floor, which the Inspector required should be preserved. The cob containing the socket had itself at some time been underpinned down to the top of the lintel, in rubble stone. It was possible, therefore, temporarily to support this cob section at its junction with the old packing rubble (Fig 185), remove the packing stones (Fig 186), slide in the steel and then pack up and make good again in rubble (Figs 187 and 188). During this operation the socket in the cob was filled with expanded polyurethane foam and the whole 'lump' of wall suspended from above within a padded cradle (Fig 186). The natural homogeneity of cob makes this sort of approach feasible and, as the record shows, it was accomplished with considerable skill by the masons.

The method of passing steel bars through the wall thickness to support a mass of cob above (see Fig 185) had been developed earlier when a lintel to a window in the south range had been replaced, effectively 'needling' at close centres.

REPAIRS AND REINSTATEMENTS TO THE NORTHERN AND WESTERN BOUNDARY WALLS

The former walls of the lost northward extension of the West Range had largely disappeared though foundations were located (Fig 189). It seems likely this range was mostly built of cob. Collapse may have been due to lack of maintenance or even abandonment. Two sections of (possibly later) cob wall survive as a garden wall of 7' to 8' (2.1mm–2.4mm) high. These needed levelling at the heads to accept correctly detailed weatherings and also some face consolidation. The wall top was very irregular, quick completion was required and the work was to be done during the winter. A system of building up in overlapping slates bedded in a mix of quick-setting hydraulic, and non-hydraulic, lime mortar was therefore

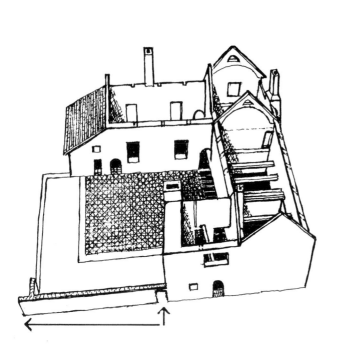

Figure 189 Location diagram of west and north boundary walls to courtyard.

Figure 191 Courtyard wall top on stripping covering to reveal degraded cob.

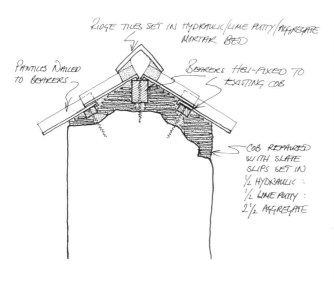

Figure 190 Richard Baker's courtyard boundary wall-head detail – reduced.

Figure 192 Courtyard wall, building up in slates and hydraulic-lime mortar, spanning gaps.

recommended and the work was successfully carried out by masons Charles Smith and Mary Jordan (Fig 190). By tailoring the size of each slate there was minimum disturbance to the existing fabric (Figs 191 and 192). On this occasion the use of a hybrid non-hydraulic / hydraulic-lime mortar mix proved entirely satisfactory. Subsequently and elsewhere difficulties have arisen. In June 1997 English Heritage recommended that a moratorium be placed on the use of hybrid mortars pending the outcome of further research.

6   Daub repairs, plasters and renders

Infill panels are one of the trickiest problems of conserva-
tion, perhaps only to be finally solved by reverting to
traditional wattle and daub.

(Charles 1990, 130)

DAUB REPAIRS

Daub repairs and reinstatements: an introduction

The particular West Country varieties of daub construction originally used at Bowhill were discussed in Chapter
2. The photo-record deals with the placing of clay-daub,
containing no chalk or lime, between and through
double-lathing in the partition wall between Great Hall
and Great Chamber (Fig 193). It involves pressing down
within, and extruding out material between lathing, and
then carrying it up over the outside of the laths as an
integral external coat. A small amount of this type of
original daub survived. An alternative, in which the wall
core is filled with daub and then plastered up externally
in a separate operation has already been discussed and is
found in the lower part of the partition between Great and
Inner Chambers. The reinstatement of both systems was
undertaken at Bowhill and is described below.

Both types of walling had suffered massive damage and
loss of fabric. Basically more fragile than cob, the integral
finish panel had been damaged by the later insertion of
openings and, most unfortunately, aborted initial
conservation works to the Great Chamber roof structure
(Fig 194). The reasons behind the loss of infill and finish
in the second panel are less clear. This was in its turn a
seventeenth-century replacement of an original,
presumably similar, arrangement.

There are no known, useful documentary records of
how the integration of lathing and daub in double-lath
panels was managed. At Bowhill the walls in question
both possessed the equivalent of top plates, so ramming
the core down in some way or other from the side was
unavoidable. It was essential that the core material should
be properly compacted as relatively solid infilling was
needed to help give these sections of walling stability
against racking. As noted elsewhere, there was no bracing
between wall-posts and plates (eaves-purlins) in original
wall framing, where this occurred at Bowhill.

In these circumstances, the approach adopted by the
Bowhill masons was to work with full lath on one side of
the wall and staged lathing on the other. Daub was placed
into the core from the open side and punned down using
a short stick (Figs 195 and 196). It was extruded out
through the laths on both sides and then beaten out over

*Figure 193 Reinstatement location: the daub panel between the Great
Hall and Great Chamber.*

them (Fig 197). This exterior material was supplemented
by adding more from the outside (see Fig 9).

The partition between Great Hall and Great Chamber

The framed panelling involved, at the first floor between
Great Hall and Great Chamber, was 17'6" (5.3m) long by
9' 0" (2.74m) high overall. On the Great Hall side daub
had originally covered all the framing, both main and
subsidiary timbers and lathing. On the Great Chamber
side the wall was formed of six separate panel bays of three
over three, divided up by main structural posts and horizontal mid-rails. The intermediate studs on the one side, and all
the framing on the other, were clad over both sides with new
riven-oak lath nailed to the timbers. As indicated above most
of the original daub and lath had been lost but a small
section remained to show correct thickness and form.

Alfred Howard's panel

During the works training session held in July 1990,
Alfred Howard directed the daubing of one of the six
Great Chamber panels (see Fig 199). At this early stage the
detailed nature, and progress, of the earth repairs was not
being monitored. Comparatively speaking, therefore,
the stiffness of the mix used is not known. This is, in the
event, unfortunate since extremely good results were
achieved under Alfred Howard's skilled tutelage. It is
possible that the daub was used drier and that its surface
was less 'worked up' than in later work. The panel was
pressed-back a couple of times as it dried, to reduce
cracking. In the end it developed a network of shrinkage
cracks similar in size and distribution to those found in
much equivalent, historic, daub. Following traditional

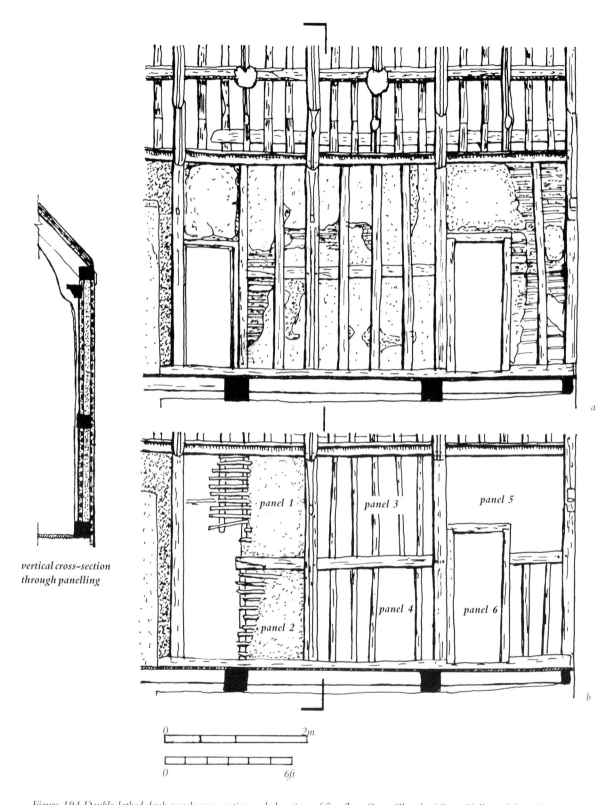

vertical cross-section through panelling

panel 1

panel 2

panel 3

panel 4

panel 5

panel 6

a

b

0   2m

0   6ft

Figure 194 Double-lathed daub-panel: cross-section and elevations of first-floor Great Chamber/Great Hall panel from Great Chamber side; (a) before any intervention, repair or reconstruction; (b) with later alterations partly removed, and, to left, surviving original lath and daub. Based on records made by Exeter Archaeology for English Heritage.

lime plastering practice wet sacking had been hung over the daub with the intention of slowing drying-out, as the weather was very hot throughout the exercise. Subsequent daub works here were carried out in October, November and early December 1990 and for these the sacking was dispensed with.

Removing stone from the raw material

For integral face daub, as here, it is important that the size of stone or gravel in the mix should not exceed the thickness of the facing daub to be carried over the laths. Ideally the largest aggregate in the mix should be 'lost' in

Figure 195 Double-lathed panel construction, Frank Lawrence punning down daub, laths removed for access, 1991.

Figure 196 Tools. Top left: sticks and 'baggers' for placing and beating out daub. Centre left: cranked sticks for ramming daub and cob blocks etc. Bottom left: wood 'floats'. Top right: mortar rake, pointing iron. Centre right: render casting shovels. Bottom right: churn brush. 1991.

the finish depth. Some aggregate had therefore to be removed before mixing; this was first attempted by riddling. Riddling was, as noted earlier, tricky where aggregate and 'clay' were damp. Riddle mesh-size was thus increased from the initially requisitioned $^1/_4$" to $^3/_4$" (6mm–18mm). With the Bowhill soils this eased matters for staff considerably without causing major problems when it came to building. As noted earlier, the removal of aggregate must increase the effect of the clay element in the mix, a fact pointed out by Adam Mackenzie, then Regional Superintendent, when the daub subsequently crazed on drying.

Daubing

The October 1990 specification called for the daub to be finished 'by steel float trowelling to both sides' (Architect's Requisition 5th October 1990, 1, item 6). The first panel daubed, following this advice, began to fail the day after placing. On the Great Hall side slumping of the wet daub was evident in the lower half of the wall. This appeared as a sag-shaped crack about 9" (225mm) long, bulging a little below. Throughout the panel-surface there were small shallow recessed areas with finite edges produced by the steel trowelling.

At the resulting emergency post-mortem site meeting it was agreed that an over-wet mix had been used. The work had, as requested, also been brought out to a square overall face, and this produced too much cover-depth over some of the riven lathing. Of its nature riven lath does not produce the squared surface offered by sawn lath. The use of a steel-trowel finish had also brought fine clay to the surface, effectively the equivalent of laitence in concrete; with this came the potential for fine cracking

of the surface as the clay dried. It was clear that trowelling and squaring-up were mistakes. As to the over-wet daub, the site workers' view was that wet material had been essential for the trowelling and squaring-up to work at all.

The revised specification simply noted that a maximum of, say, 1" (25mm) cover to laths should be achieved. Since the lathing was not all on the same plane the finished daub surface would not be perfectly regular. Daub was to be put in by hand from both sides, rammed into the core and thrown and beaten-in at the face, the latter by means of a 'bagger', a rectangular timber block with curved leading and rear edges and a cranked, parallel handle (see Fig 196). Smoothing, for a plane finish, was to be avoided. These application methods would allow the use of a drier mix.

For a typical framed panel, a sixth of the total, the site team reckoned to need between 20 and 24 builders' buckets of infill daub and a further 14 or so for exterior application. One day was required to prepare and one day to place this amount of material. Both sides of the panels were fully lathed-up. A series of laths were then removed from one side, sufficient to allow room for the punning-down of material to the depth of the ramming-in stick (see Fig 195). When the filling operation was complete the missing laths were carefully screwed back to avoid disturbing the original daub and the process repeated. New, and original, laths were in short lengths, making the refixing job straightforward. In beating the daub out over the laths externally the bagger was worked with sliding, angled blows to move material over to cover the laths and indentations arising from concentrations of hay in the mix (see Fig 197). A plain finished surface resulted. Cover to the laths varied somewhat. Towards the base of the new work on the Great Hall side, and over

Figure 197 Double-lathed panel, beating back daub extruded out after punning down as shown in Figure 196, 1990.

Figure 199 Double-lathed panel reconstruction, daubing in progress, Great Chamber side. Lower left panel is Alfred Howard's completed trial work; above this is remaining original daub. The original timber armature construction had to be largely replaced, outside the patch of historic daub, 1991.

the main posts on this side, daub was successfully carried over lathing fixed direct to the surface of substantial timbers. Figure 200 shows work in progress on the side facing the Great Hall. Figure 199 shows completed work from the Great Chamber side, including lime plaster trials to the lower left and right hand panels.

Drying-out shrinkage-cracking

Over about a month (November 1990) the partition was completely daubed-out. On the Great Chamber side two panels were lime plastered very shortly after finishing. These experiments are described below. Elsewhere, other than in the panel containing the section of original daub, the material was left to dry out with minimal aftercare (at

most one pressing-back of cracking), as it was felt that, traditionally, not much time would have been spent on this (Fig 200). On the Great Hall side the whole wall was completed as a continuous daubed surface over all framing timbers. By early December 1991 shrinkage on this side was generally confined to network cracking with sub-structure formation showing through as cracking in a few places (Fig 201). The bays left fair-faced on the Great Chamber side showed similar failures by this time. Failure overall was noticeably greater than for Alfred Howard's control panel, which was a disappointment (Fig 202). A month later, in early February 1991, shrinkage cracking had developed further. Some original, major, cracks were now up to $1/4$" (6mm) wide though most were less. Within the major fracture zones hairline

Figure 198 Double-lathed panel reconstruction, daub preparation and daubing work to the Great Hall side of the screen, in progress; daubing, mixing and placing new daub on the storage heap, 1990 (Mark Joy, Frank Lawrence and trainee).

Figure 200 Double-lathed panel reconstruction, the completed repaired and reinstated daub panels, Great Chamber side; panel 1: original and new daub (top left); panel 2: Alfred Howard's panel with trial plaster (bottom left); panels 3 and 4: new daub that has had no 'aftercare' (top and bottom centre); panels 5 and 6: two new daub panels with plaster applied to the wet daub (right), 1990.

cracks had appeared. Large-scale cupping, slight curling-up of edges of cracks, surrounding 'islands' of daub, was evident throughout. Internal failure was in most places not of such an extent as to detach surface material completely from its background. This did, however, finally happen on the Great Hall side where three areas of daub (maximum approximate size each 2'0" x 1'6" x 2" or 0.6m x 0.45m x 50mm, deep) eventually became loose, where they lay on lathing fixed over solid timbering at the base of the wall.

It is likely that a number of factors contributed to the failures described. The raw soil employed was the same as that used by Alfred Howard for the first trial. While, therefore, batching-in extra sand would have helped, it may not have been strictly necessary. The material was probably still over-wet when applied; the stiffer the daub, the harder it is to work it. Fibre (hay) content may not have been at the optimum. The method of finishing may not have been ideal. On this last point, the moving about of the surface section of the daub in covering over the laths may have induced extra stresses into the finish, producing more failures. More pressing-back aftercare, as had been applied to a small degree to Alfred Howard's panel, would certainly have helped.

In spite of the extent of failure eventually developed in the face of the daub, it was considered sufficiently sound to be left in place and, at most, made good. That on the Great Chamber side was to be lime plastered following evidence of the original use of this finish in that location. That on the Great Hall side was to be finished fair-faced and limewashed, again following original (or at any rate, earlier) evidence. It was decided that plastering would be sufficient to seal the cracks on the Great Chamber side (other than for panels 5 and 6, see below). These also offered a key to the plaster. The cracks on the Great Hall side, however, had to be made good before limewashing.

Figure 202 Double-lathed panel reconstruction, Great Chamber, detail of daubing: below is Alfred Howard's daub panel; above new daub is matched to existing grouted, original, daub. Note that the new daub has been rubbed back to control shrinkage, action not taken in the adjoining two panels (to far right beyond the cruck post), 1991.

Making good cracks in the new daub, Great Hall

A 'clay plaster' developed at the site prior to 1990 had included a proportion of dung. This, it was said, had successfully improved bonding of new, wet material to already dry 'clay'. A dung-and-daub mix was therefore used to fill major cracks on the Great Hall side of the panel. Minor cracks, having no structural implications, were left to be filled later by the limewash alone. Cracks for filling were first sprayed, widened out slightly behind with the finger-trowel blade, and then plugged with a

Figure 201 Double-lathed panel reconstruction, completed panel to Great Hall showing network-cracking filled; below, with dung/clay mix and above with lime-mortar mix. Note new sloping daub ceiling-panel over Great Chamber, within roof structure, also trial limewash patches, 1991.

Figure 203 Double-lathed panel reconstruction, Mark Joy filling cracks, Great Chamber side, in preparation for limewashing direct to the daub, 1991.

fine clay and dung paste from which stone and gravel had been removed (Fig 203). A simple ribbon test had been done on the raw soil before use, to check its suitability for the purpose (see Norton 1986, 17). All the samples tested fell within a safe range. Following filling, the crack areas were rubbed back a couple of times over two days, as they began to open on drying. This helped to reduce a little the surface cupping effect described earlier, and closed them up again.

The three major loose areas referred to above were cut out and reinstated using the dung mix, but incorporating the larger aggregate that had been removed from the crack-filling material. Subsequent performance was satisfactory.

To help speed up the works, agreement was given for face-cracking to the upper parts of the wall to be filled with lime mortar (4 sand to 1 lime) rather than clay. This too was found to work satisfactorily (see Fig 201). Where a small patch of original daub showed within the new material its edges were carefully 'filletted', ie the junction between old and new was bound-in by the application of a continuous ribbon of lime mortar. The lower edge of the new daub, where it overhung the top rail of the ground floor framing below, was chamfered off when dry to a 45° angle using a hacksaw blade.

Consolidating the surviving original daub

The one surviving section of daub in the double-lath wall (panel 1) between the Great Chamber and Hall measured some 3 x 4' (0.9 x 1.2m). Particularly on the Chamber side it was badly cracked and voided and parts of the surface were loose and friable (see Fig 199). Its condition on the Hall side, relatively speaking, was better. Fragments of original plaster adhered in places.

Figure 204 Double-lathed panel reconstruction, grouting historic daub, demonstrating method of lime-grouting daub panel using vetinerary syringe. The white linear markings on the panel are grout at the panel surface, filling cracks. Below the workman's hand is a patch of original plaster, 1990.

Lathing missing from the panel was first replaced, using screws to avoid vibration dislodging the original material. The daub was then consolidated using the same lime grouting system as for detached plaster grouting.[43] The panel, being quite thick, was grouted from both sides (Fig 204).

Although this first consolidation appeared to help to hold the daub together, the surface remained in a loose and friable condition in places, especially on the Great Chamber side. With the subsequent application of new daub close to and around the original daub, the latter was loosened again a little. A second grouting was therefore carried out, mostly on the Great Chamber side, since the Great Hall side was in the end largely covered over by new daub.

Reinstating daub over and around original daub

Once the original daub had been consolidated, work began to complete the rest of the panel in new daub prepared to the same specification as before. This involved some patching over and through the original material as the photo-record shows. Mist-spraying of the medieval daub where the new was to come into contact with it was controlled so that erosion and over-softening did not occur. Procedure was the same as for the other bays but obviously more care and attention was required of the craftsmen.

The degree of shrinkage cracking in the adjoining new bay can be compared with that of the new daub in the repaired bay and also with Alfred Howard's original control bay below this if the photo-record shot (see Fig 202) is studied carefully. The reduction in cracking in the repair bay is due to aftercare, the result of 'burnishing', rubbing-back the cracking, as with Alfred Howard's bay, at intervals over a period of a week or two. When completely dry it was possible to tidy-up the join with the old by chamfering the edges of the new, using a blade, to highlight original, still intact, internal plaster. A hinged timber cover-panel was later arranged, allowing the whole bay to be viewed if desired, exactly as it was left after repair. The remaining five panels to the Great Chamber side were, as noted earlier, subsequently lime plastered (see below).

Ceiling daub: reinstatement in the plane of the roof over the Great Chamber at the junction of the Hall and South Range

This work took place within the triangle formed by the valley-boards of the Great Hall roof, (which were laid up the rafters of the South Range roof over the Great Chamber) and the related Great Chamber internal, northern eaves (cornice) plate. The South Range rafters in this area had been lathed above, and daubed between. They had been stripped of both lath and daub during the first stage of conservation (Figs 205 and 206), to allow for their repair. The daub had been carefully preserved in bags for future re-use. Similar lath-and-daub arrangements survived at the equivalent junction of South and West Ranges, though only in a fragmentary way.

Figure 205 Ceiling daub reinstatement. The original material shown here (1983) had been removed and stored by the time of the second stage works. The reinstatement involved a mix of original and new daub on the single-lathing shown above.

Figure 206 Ceiling daub reinstatement, area shown in Figure 205, viewed from below, within the Great Chamber with new laths and valley-boards, awaiting new daubing. Completed double lath daub panels below. For the completed, lime-plastered, works see Figure 228.

The laths were replaced in split-oak as before, to the same centres, leaving gaps of 1" to 1¼" (25 to 30mm) between them (Fig 206). A trial section of daub was attempted in January 1991, using daub sweepings with bigger aggregate particles removed. This proved successful enough for the full-scale operation to go forward, which it did in early May 1991. The original daub was sieved to remove bits of broken lath etc and was then reworked with water and hay in the usual way. Extra 'make-up' subsoil was taken from pre-sieved material prepared prior to the 1990 works. Three men were involved, one working from above and one below the rafters with a third following on with the plaster finish (see below). From below, the daub was divided up into narrow bays between the rafters. From above, it was finished as a continuous sheet covering everything.

Daub was applied by hand, pressing down from above with the flat of the hand and with a rolling-pin action from the short beating-stick (Fig 207). It was finally flattened out using the bagger. From below, material extruded through the laths from above was pressed back up by hand, spread out over the laths and again gently flattened with the bagger (Fig 208). Any extra material needed was added from below during this work. Beating was found to be counter-productive, loosening adjoining, completed, rafter bays. Thickness on completion averaged 1" to 1½" (25–38mm) above the laths to ¾" (18mm) below. After about an hour the underside was plastered (see below for the justification for this practice). The upper side was left fair-faced and given no further attention. Eventually it dried and the resulting shrinkage-crack pattern followed closely that recorded on photos

Figure 207 (right) Ceiling daub reinstatement. Tom Perring applying daub to top of ceiling panel, using hand and stick, to be followed by 'bagger', 1991.

Figure 208 (far right) Ceiling daub reinstatement. Charles Smith applying ceiling-daub from below, in concert with application from above (Fig 207).

Figure 209 Location diagram, double-lathed cross-screen reinstatement, first floor between Great and Inner Chambers.

taken before its removal and that of the little remaining early ceiling daub at the opposite end of the South Range (intersection with the kitchen range) (see Plate 13). The performance of the underside of the daub, between the rafters, is discussed below under finishes. It eventually failed less than the top surface, the plaster and rafter bays helping to control cracking.

The partition between the Great Chamber and Inner Chamber

By 1987, only the lower half of the infill and framing of the partition in this location, the sixteenth-century replacement of the original, survived (Fig 209). This lower section had been a double-lathed screen similar in principle to that between the Hall and Great Chamber. It differed slightly from the latter however in that an independant daub plaster had been applied over the lathed core-daub. The form of construction used in the upper part of the screen is unknown.

Nearly half the daub infill and two-thirds of the lathing had been lost from the surviving partition. On one side half the partition's daub plaster was still in place, though somewhat loosened (Fig 210). This, as noted in Chapter 2, consisted of a daub and hair mix of almost felt-like consistency, put on in two layers. To one side of the partition was the framing for a doorway.

Consolidating the partition

The first step in consolidation was to lime-grout and partially push back the loosened daub plaster. The grout was similar to that described as used in the Great Hall/ Great Chamber panel, injected into the gap between plaster and daub panel-core infill. Because here proved to be much voiding this became a laborious job, taking a week to complete. The grout, containing HTI powder, went-off quickly. It was also applied to cracks elsewhere in the panel-core daub itself to produce a more solid,

bedded, material. (For full details of the mix and processes used again here see endnote 43).

Grouting completed, the missing areas of lath-work and the missing core-daub were reinstated satisfactorily. The laths were fixed using stainless steel screws, again so as to avoid shaking the existing material loose. The missing upper part of the panel was then studded out to the apex, and lathed on both sides for lime plaster. It was decided not to carry the daub work higher. At this stage the door-frame proper was reinstated.

The new daub plaster to the partition.

Experiment with different daub plaster mixes to complete the finish to the double lath wall was carried out next. Trial patches of hair-bound daub plaster comprising straight sieved raw earth, the same with clay strength reduced by the addition of sand and then with 5% hydrated lime added, were applied to the completed daub and lathing when the latter had hardened sufficiently. At the small scale of the experiment the straight mix was judged, on drying, to perform best (Fig 211). The trial patches were done in early October 1992 and full daub plastering was complete by the end of the month. This is quite a good time of year to be plastering as the heat of the sun is in decline.

The process of manufacture of the new daub plaster was as follows:

- prepare the raw subsoil, dry, and passed through a 3mm sieve.
- spread out a layer of subsoil.
- sprinkle on hair, in this case goat's hair.[44]
- spread another thin layer of subsoil.
- sprinkle more hair etc.
- turn the lot over, add water carefully and mix to a thick paste (not too much water)
- use immediately (Fig 212).

Charles Smith noted that the hair 'springs out when you have incorporated as much as possible'. Going by the appearance of the original daub plaster, the mixing-in of as much hair as the earth would take, became the aim. A final, straight raw-earth patch was therefore prepared with the absolute maximum of hair in it and, on proving satisfactory, this became the control mix.

Because the old daub 'kept sucking the moisture out of the repairs', the background was well wetted the day before daubing, an hour before and then at the time of application. The daub was put on at an average of ⅝" (15mm) thick, in one coat, wood-floated to the contours of the wall (the original daub was two-coat work, to the same total thickness). The steel float was found to close-up the surface, producing laitence, probably slowing drying and with the possibility of crazing.

The daub plaster went on easily, but needed aftercare. For the first week after completion (early November 1992), as the material was setting, cracks were sprayed up and trowelled back each day as they developed (Figs 213 and 214). During the second week, pressing-back with a dry trowel was found to be all that was necessary. After this, with the exception of a small control area (discussed below), there was no more aftercare nor was this really necessary. Subsequent cracking was very fine-scale and easily lost in the coatings of limewash that followed (Fig 215).

The control area, defined by four drawing pins, continued to be rubbed back whenever cracking appeared, until the material became solid. As implied above, and as the photo-record shows, however, although here the failures were further reduced, comparatively speaking there was no real benefit in extending this operation in this particular case. It is of some interest that this process of pressing-back cracking, known also as burnishing, has been used at other times and by other peoples, notably the ancient Chinese who thereby produced sculpture from subsoil having a clay content well in excess of what we would normally consider useable (pers comm John Warren).

In terms of performance and aesthetic the daub plasterwork appeared to be entirely successful. If tapped, the places where it spanned the vertical studwork, rang hollow. But there was no failure, the hair holding the finish together everywhere as intended.

Figure 210 (right) Double-lathed cross-screen reinstatement, prior to works. All laths removed on this side as far down as the daub plaster. The daub infill stands without support, 1990.

Figure 211 (far right) Double-lathed cross-screen reinstatement, detail of new replacement laths to cross-screen with new daub-infill behind. The three patch areas are differing mix trials for the new daub plaster. The new daub infill background is dry, 1992.

Figure 212 (right) Double-lathed cross-screen, haired daub-plaster after preparation, 1992.

Figure 213 (far right) Double-lathed cross-screen, detail of haired daub-plaster showing effect of hair 'sprung' from the surface as well as cracking in process of trowelling back, 1992.

Figure 214 (right) Double-lathed cross-screen, completed daub-plaster during drying, 1992. Lath and lime plaster panel above.

Figure 215 (far right) Double-lathed cross-screen, daub repair to original daub-plaster at door-frame, showing surface hair 'lost' in successive limewash coatings, 1993.

Figure 216 Renders of various types and ages on the courtyard walls at Bowhill, late 1940s/early 1950s. (Copyright: A W Everett).

RENDER AND PLASTER

Original lime renders and plasters at Bowhill

For the purposes of what follows, external wall finishes are referred to as renders, and internal as plasters. Much of the original plaster and all but a tiny fraction of the original render coatings at Bowhill had been lost (Fig 216). The history of the site's finishes appeared to be the replacement of high quality by more vernacular and finally by modern finishes (Blaylock forthcoming). This progression would reflect the vicissitudes of the building's history of use. In the final stage of its history, following acquisition by the state, it seems that a decision was made to strip all internal finishes back to what remained of the original medieval plaster. This process can be seen completed in the first floor, South Range, in a works photograph taken in 1978 (Fig 217). By 1987, the second-stage works, the exterior had been almost entirely covered in modern cement renders and these were mostly removed, revealing bare fabric.

It seems likely that there was originally little if any difference in the composition of external render and internal plaster, given, as indicated in the archaeological report, that both will have been drawn from the same supply source as the mortar for the masonry (Blaylock forthcoming).

The make-up of surviving original plaster sampled by the Exeter Archaeological Field Unit (EMAFU, now

Exeter Archaeology) did not appear to vary much whether applied over stone or cob. It contained white lime and grit, often a range of grits, from fine to coarse and visibly angular, as well as the odd pebble. It was one-coat work, following the wall's contours and thus varying in thickness between 1/8" and 1/2" (3 and 12mm), a sensible approach since where cob is concerned, the lighter the finish the better. The fair-face of an earth wall is always weaker than even the softest sand/lime render coat subsequently applied to it. To perform satisfactorily such a finish is likely to be denser, and therefore heavier, by equivalent volume, than its earthern background. Received wisdom has it that applied protective coatings to earth walls should ideally be as weak as the wall itself. This is the case with the classic vernacular finish to earth walls, earth and earth/dung renders, acting as sacrificial coverings to be regularly renewed. The same goes for limewash straight to the wall, at least until many re-coatings build up its weight, and tar which was commonly used on the 'clay-lump' walls of nineteenth-century East Anglian tradition. Weakness is argued as the ideal, for reasons of mechanical bond and moisture-vapour permeability: the thinner the material the longer it will take to pull off the wall under its own weight, and the less dense the easier it will be for vapour to pass through it.

The medieval plaster had invariably been painted over with limewash, generally recorded as white, but in at least one case red. In places this primary plaster was found to have been hacked to provide a key for secondary plaster,

Figure 217 Later plasters stripped in the South Range, first floor, to expose areas of original medieval plaster beneath, 1987. (Photograph: Exeter Archaeology)

applied over it at a later date. This second coat was very different in composition from the first.[45]

One very interesting feature was noticed in relation to a sample of remaining original plaster to the daubed double-lath panelling between the Great Chamber and Hall. The record reads as follows:

> *112 (ii) Surface skim of 1st floor Chamber/Hall partition, s.face.* Primary late-med type lime mortar, approx 7–8mm thick; thin skim or wash on outer surface; deep red cob adhering to rear face. Quite coarse for thickness in the sense that the mix contains pebbles larger in diameter than the thickness of the plastering (Blaylock forthcoming).

In the normal way of things the occasional piece of oversized aggregate would have been flicked out by the mason during plastering. Close inspection of other surviving plaster from this location confirmed that some aggregates, coated all over with lime, were embedded into the daub background (Fig 218). It therefore seemed possible that these particular panels had been plastered while the daub was still plastic. In such circumstances, some too-large diameter aggregate may have been accommodated by pushing it into the still soft background. As a result of these observations, experiments with plastering to damp daub were made; these are described below. The discovery is a good example of the careful examination of existing fabric yielding clues as to former

working methods. (Such treatment, incidentally, would not have been appropriate over mass cob. Daub is usually smoothly homogenous, due to the removal of gravel and stone. Cob, on the other hand, can contain these ingre-

Figure 218 Original daub double-lathed first floor panel between Great Chamber and Hall. Close-up detail of face of original daub to double-lath panelling (section of lath at top). Some original plaster survives and some aggregate from this has been 'rolled' into the daub background, 1990.

Figure 219 Example of one mid 1980s English Heritage trial daub-plaster mix (with its recipe scratched into its surface) over cob, kitchen wall, 1990.

dients in abundance, making attempts to press in large aggregate within a finish rather difficult.)

Few possible pointers to the nature of the original exterior lime render survived by the time of the EMAFU survey. When the wall of the early nineteenth-century framed cottage, partly abutting the west gable of Bowhill, was taken down for repair, a large patch of later cob/lime render over original cob was revealed. A sample was removed by the Unit and the relevant comment in the record is as follows:

> 404. a fragment of lime mortar adhering to the rear face of the large sample may be remains of an earlier exterior render; this would appear to be standard late-med mix outer surface? scored for adherence of surface skim (Blaylock forthcoming).

Cob/lime plaster experiments before 1987

Information from Adam MacKenzie and Robin Court (masons) throws some light on experimental plastering at the site prior to 1987. It will be remembered that a number of trial plaster panels onto cob remained from this period on the Kitchen internal south wall (Fig 219). The finishes derived from these and ultimately used in the Great Hall were varied for different backgrounds: over stonework, an approximately 1:2 mix of lime putty and silver sand, sometimes with the addition of a small quantity of brick-dust and hair. Over cob a relatively weak mix (about 1:5) of lime, sieved earth and red sharp sand, with small amounts of dung and chopped hay, all trodden-in. In the latter case, the lime element would be a major determinant of the performance of the mix. There is insufficient information about the way in which adding dung benefits the plastering process for any useful discussion to be developed here. The cob/lime plaster averaged half an inch in thickness and cracking was dealt

with by wetting down and rubbing back over the course of a week.

The consolidation of existing plaster and render

Everywhere, on both cob and stone, mortar 'fillets' were applied to the edges of surviving patches of original lime and other early plasters and renders. This has been standard Ancient Monuments practice with historic finishes over stone for many years. Where the finish to be treated was very weak, it was first lightly sprayed with limewater, an operation repeated throughout the whole of one day. The application of limewater, calcium-carbonate saturated water from the top of the putty-lime pit or tub, is thought to strengthen friable finishes.[46] The mortar used for the fillets comprised $1:2\frac{1}{2}$ (lime:sand). At Bowhill the fillets were intended to bind-in the edges of isolated patches of finish, securing them against damage, including water uptake, when new plaster/render was brought up to and around them, and sealing their edges where grouting was to follow. Application involved fine-spraying the background with limewater again, working the fillet around and into exposed edges, and splaying it down from these to the raw wall surface. The fillets were given a textured finish (Fig 220). Any grouting, ie internal re-bonding of plaster or render, or of these to the wall, was done using the standard English Heritage grout mix injected by veterinary syringe (described in endnote 43) once the fillets had gone off. Particularly fragile-surfaced material was shelter-coated for extra protection, using the fillet mortar mix strained through a very fine sieve, to which was added liquid made from equal parts of skimmed milk and water, the milk being mildly adhesive when dry. The whole was then painted over with thin limewash.

Figure 220 Background preparation for finishes, example of the filleting of the edges of historic plaster to protect and tie it in before new plaster and render are brought up to it. The original plaster around a jointed-cruck post in the Oriel Chamber is c 1500.

Figure 221 Scat. Scat-casting using a shortened coal shovel. From Bedford et al 1993. (Copyright: DEBA and Larry Keefe)

Alfred Howard's training session: 'scat'

Alfred Howard came to Bowhill on 28 September 1990 to demonstrate the application of Devon scat onto the first double-lath daub trial panel (panel 2) in the Great Chamber, completed under his direction in the summer and by then appearing stable enough to take a finish. The Inspector recorded the event thus:

* he wetted the wall.
* he threw on the scat (fine grit in a wet lime slurry) using a scat implement (Fig 221) backhand with a flicking action from the wrist.

Figure 223 Finishes to new daub, double lathed first floor panel between Hall and Great Chamber: panels 1 and 2. Note the remnant of original daub with some of its plaster, in panel 1. At the foot of the replacement panel (panel 2) is Alfred Howard's patch of scat/trowelled finish, a part of which had been dealt with as one-coat work by Francis Kelly as a test to match (apparent) evidence of the original plaster on daub in the panel above, 1991.

* he paused and stood back for about 30 seconds.
* he applied a further coat of 1:3 (lime:aggregate) with a metal trowel and smoothed it back (also working backhand).

Best practice calls for the scat undercoat to dry but not 'set' before application of the finish coat or coats (Fig 222). (See Charles Smith's comment in endnote 48.) Alfred Howard telescoped two operations here for demonstration purposes but, in the event, the finished area remained sound (Fig 223).

It is instructive to compare this modern but no doubt time-honoured practical example with a 1921 Devon description of rough-casting, where a hot mix of lime and grit is cast, or thrown, onto wet render as a final, external finish. [47] This technique, but not using the lime hot, is today known as harling in the northern parts of Britain.

Figure 222 Scat. Detail of 'gone off' scat undercoat applied by Alfred Howard to a demonstration lath-and-daub panel at a Bowhill training day in 1990. The effect of the force of the casting is visible in the spatter of lime and grit from the daub over the lath at the top of the illustration. The daub was not fully dry when scatting took place, 1990. (Copyright: Ray Harrison)

Figure 224 (above left) Finishes to new daub, Great Chamber, close up of ridging of grits in plaster, corner of panel 5, 1991.

Figure 225 (above right) Finishes to new daub, Great Chamber, contrasting panels 5 and 6. The lower panel shows amended plaster mix. Some cracking is visible in the plaster but this did not develop to any degree, 1991.

Figure 226 (left) Finishes to new daub, Great Chamber, view of completed panels 5 and 6. The plaster in the top panel is drying out. Lower panel with brown earth-stains from background showing as a result of less advanced drying out, 1991.

In both cases the force of throwing on either the render keying-coat or finish is intended to aid adherence, a point well brought out in the extract from a talk given to SPAB by the late Rex Gardiner (date unknown), part of which advises that depending on the type of cob it is sometimes worthwhile to aid keying by giving a splash coat of strong cement and sand before rendering, clearly not something we would recommend today.

Alfred Howard's thrown lime mortar scratch-coat is the more conservation- and building-friendly (and no doubt traditional) version of Gardiner's cement and sand splash-coat. Both are, as Gardiner says, an aid to keying to the weak background offered by cob. The essential point here is the clear Devon preference for applying the thrown scat/splash-coat first, to key between the weak background and the stronger lime/sand finish coat. This preference appears to apply primarily to external renders, which are subject to greater weathering extremes than internal finishes.

Alfred Howard's common-sense and traditional view of all this repeats that cob will 'slough' any external coating unless it is keyed and unless its thickness is kept down (pers comm Francis Kelly). As we saw earlier, in some parts of the country, notably under recent tradition the New Forest, evidence of this argument carried to a logical conclusion can still be seen in cob protected externally not by render but by limewash alone, applied direct to the earth. Needless to say, evidence of this practice is also to be found in Devon.

The first Great Chamber plaster trials to daub

Alfred Howard's demonstration of scat to panel 2 of the six double-lathed daub panels in the dividing wall between the Great Chamber and Hall was followed by the plastering of the remaining panels (see Fig 200 for location of panels 1 to 6). As we have seen, it had been concluded from the evidence that the panels had originally been plastered to

Figure 227 Finishes to new ceiling daub, Frank Lawrence applying plaster to damp daub with the gauging trowel, 1991 (see endnote 49).

Figure 228 Finishes to new ceiling daub, view of completed works (skim of plaster onto wet daub), 1991.

wet daub. This was therefore the approach chosen for panels 5 and 6. Working again from the original evidence the use of one-coat work, trowelled straight on, was decided on. This approach was confirmed as a result of successful experiment with one-coat, one-action application of lime plaster to dry cob adjacent to Alfred Howard's demonstration patch, omitting the scat stage.

Completion of daubing to the Great Chamber side of panel 5 (and then panel 6) was thus followed by immediate application of a 1:3 lime plaster made up of one part unsieved lime putty, one part sand (Wilmington – local source) and two parts washed beach shingle (aggregate size $^1/_8$"–$^3/_{16}$", or 3–5mm, maximum). The masons had no difficulty in laying the lime plaster onto the daub, but the larger aggregate in the mix ridged slightly in the finished work (Fig 224). For panel 6, therefore, treated in the same way but some 24 hours after the daub was complete, the plaster composition was amended. On the advice of Adam MacKenzie, Regional Superintendent, the largest aggregate was omitted and the balance altered to 1° lime putty : 1 sand : 2 grit; workability and final finish were both thereby improved, as can be seen from Figure 225.

There were two, at this stage unanticipated, results of plastering directly to wet daub. One was the immediate intermixing, and presumably therefore bonding, of plaster and background, evidenced in the brown earth-stains that quickly rose through to the surface of the wet plaster in places (Fig 226). The other related to shrinkage cracking in the daub itself. It will be remembered that there was extensive network, contraction, cracking in daub panels 3 and 4, which were allowed to go off solid before plastering. By contrast, surface contraction cracking through the integral plaster to panels 5 and 6 was in the end negligible. This suggests that the relationship between wet daubs and plasters is worth detailed examination under more controlled conditions. The success of the trial was enough in this case to justify the use of the same approach for plastering the underside of the newly daubed ceiling panels in the Great Chamber (Fig 227) described earlier. Here shrinkage in the integral lime plaster surfacing to the daub finally showed as horizontal cracks spaced out quite regularly between the rafters (Fig 228). These were easily filled subsequently with lime slurry. Again, as noted earlier, the top of the daub, continuous above the rafters, eventually showed the usual network shrinkage-crack pattern of similar fair-faced daub elsewhere.

There remained those panels 3 and 4 and parts of 2, where the daub was fully gone-off before plastering. These were heavily sprayed with water to soften the background a little to help bonding and to control drying-out of mortar. They were then plastered direct with the same one-coat mix (Figs 229 and 230). Results, again, were satisfactory. The strong network cracking in the daub offered a good key for the plaster.

Choice of internal plaster to cob

The usual dubbing-out of, and making-good to, wall faces, before plastering, was done using cob, or cob-lime, or lime mortar (Fig 231). Processes involving cob and cob-lime have already been considered. No problems were encountered in dubbing-out small shallow areas of cob with lime mortar alone subject to the usual saturation of the background. On the whole, though, filling in cob or cob/lime mortar is probably to be preferred as, apart from their similar material properties, their density, and therefore weight, is less than that of pure sand/lime.

A number of wall sockets, whose configuration had to be protected for archaeological reasons, were filled with small reclaimed stones bedded in cob-lime mortar. Packing of some of the partly voided chases against the jointed cruck posts of the South Range north wall was managed similarly, using lime mortar. This followed original practice, except that in the original the packing stones were bedded in a mix of earth and lime mortars.

Figure 229 Finishes to new daub, Frank Lawrence spraying up the dry panels 3 and 4, Great Chamber, 1992.

Figure 230 Finishes to new daub, applying plaster to wetted panel 4, Frank Lawrence plastering with a wooden float, 1992. Note the network cracking, here and in Figure 229.

Examination of the quite extensive areas of surviving plaster over cob within the South Range had suggested that the original material was relatively lime-rich (Blaylock forthcoming). Following the 1:3 mix plaster trials to the double-lathed panels a small experiment with a 1:2½ mix was carried out on the east side of the new cob cross-wall. The results appearing satisfactory, the approved mix for all further plastering and rendering was agreed as 1:2½ (lime putty:aggregate). The latter comprised 80% yellow/white Devon Rockbeare coarse sand and 20% Rockbeare 6mm 'rounds'. This was applied in one coat, averaging rather less than ½" (12mm) thick. The approach to plastering at the site was essentially the same as for external rendering, described below.

External rendering and internal plastering to cob

In the light of the archaeological evidence, sparse as it was, it was decided to extend the idea of the one-coat, light-weight render to the building's exterior, in similar mix proportions, ie 1:2½ lime putty:aggregate (coarse stuff), to that already used within; this method is in contrast to the vernacular Devon scat keying-coat practice described above.

The works approach to this rendering was developed out of experiment on site, from experience of working with lime mortars. The render team, led by SPAB William Morris Craft Fellow Charles Smith, having been set the target of applying one-coat exterior render, found their own means of managing shrinkage on widely differing backgrounds with widely differing suction rates.

Rendering was commenced, over cob and stone, on the east elevation of the Hall. This had been limewashed direct under the pre-1987 works. The limewash was successfully washed off by carefully controlled pressure spraying. The condition of the modern cob-lime element

here was such that new finishes could be applied without any need to make good, or dub-out, its surface. Elsewhere, for instance with the original cob of the south elevation, surface stabilization was needed before rendering. This was done by giving an initial coating of lime slurry to the wall as a surface consolidant (Fig 233). The general procedures adopted inside and out were to brush down the exposed wall face lightly to remove the worst surface dust and spallings.

The background, if in reasonable condition, as were most of the interior cob wall faces, was saturated by thoroughly spraying 24 hours before, one hour before and then immediately before the application of plaster/render. When spraying-up internally, lime water was used because the masons felt it would add a little hardening to the wall faces.

Alternatively, old, more surface-degraded cob and some stonework was given a priming coat of putty-lime slurry to stablize its friable nature. This involved a coat of thin lime-slurry well brushed into the surface. The process was as follows: wet the surface first, paint on the lime slurry so that it combines with the cob. Allow to dry and apply render coat on the same day. If slurry is allowed to go hard, ie to fully set, then a shear plane is caused and bonding the render coat is difficult. If it does become too dry then the slurry must be sprayed lightly with water before rendering [48] (Figs 232 and 233).

The plastering/rendering material used was coarse stuff (the basic mortar and plaster mix consisting of 1:2½ lime putty: aggregate). It was remixed that day, using the Rolpanit™ mortar mill (Fig 234), after standing for at least three weeks in storage bays, laid-up as thin as possible and then pushed very well in. This was done with normal plastering tools but with emphasis on the gauging trowel.[49] As the photo record suggests, this is hard work (Fig 235). The wall contours were closely followed.

Figure 231 (above) Finishes to cob, filling and making good in lime mortar to gaps to sides of jointed-cruck posts and beneath cornice plate, Inner Chamber, 1993.

Figure 232 (above right) Finishes to cob, Boysel Welham applying lime slurry prior to plastering, 1993.

Figure 233 (right) Finishes to cob, partly dry lime slurry intended to stabilize cob background, exterior of South Range, 1993.

Figure 234 Finishes to cob, Rolpanit™ mixer, Bowhill: Boysel Welham remixing 'coarse stuff' for render, 1993.

Figure 235 Finishes to cob, general view with Mike Perrett at work, note the dampened (lime) cob background, 1993. North lean-to extension to Hall.

Figure 236 Finishes to cob, Charles Smith 'banging back' with a
bristle brush, 1993.

Figure 238 Finishes to cob, Charles Smith using distemper brush for
final finish, 1993.

Figure 237 Finishes to cob, contrast the 'banged back' area to right
with newly trowelled material showing crack, 1993.

As the plaster dried, cracks were compacted with a
'churn-brush' (a stiff bristle brush), and trowelled over.
This might need doing between three and four times as
the plaster hardened.

In the case of the render, almost immediately after
laying-on and perhaps twice or three times in the day,
as the render set and cracks developed, it was compacted back, as above, by banging with a stiff bristle-
brush leaving a stippled face. There was no further
trowelling. The use of the bristle-brush only is an alternative to rubbing-up, ie pressing-in cracks with the
trowel as they develop, and was preferred external
practice (Fig 236).

Each time an area of render was compacted back it was
painted over using a wet distemper brush. This gave the
required finish, ie following the contours, smooth but not
too polished, and kept the surface from drying-out too
quickly (Figs 237 and 238).

For plaster the drying time internally varied, averaging two days to reach the stage where more working-
over could break the bond with the cob.

Externally, within from a day to a week, depending on
atmospheric moisture levels, there would again come a
point where any further compacting would start to
break the render's bond with the wall. It then had to
stop.

Any hair-line cracks that subsequently developed
were stopped by a final finish of thick slurry from the
bottom of the limewash bucket. It was sometimes necessary to paint this over two or three times as final set took
place.

Limewash should then ideally be applied before the
render has fully dried out, for maximum bond, and to
slow the render's drying time further. (pers comm Charles
Smith).

It is axiomatic with lime plaster and renders that rapid
drying causes sudden volume changes, ie sudden shrinkage and therefore cracking. Slowing the drying process
can help to reduce such cracking. Apart from pressing in
developing cracks as just described, conventional lime
mortar practice attempts to protect 'green' areas of plaster
from the elements and to control drying speed. This is
often done, in warm weather, by shading the wall with
hessian, and by wetting this sacking at intervals to cool the
air, at the wall face, and to reduce evaporation: this was
the practice externally at Bowhill. At the time of writing
there is no sign of any serious shrinkage-cracking externally or internally over cob, though one or two areas do
ring hollow. Subsequently an investigation by the BRE
of the external render concluded that this hollowness was
due to the background de-laminating rather than render-
bond failure.

Figure 239 Finishes to cob, sketch of the effect of 'banging back' with a stiff brush. (Copyright: Charles Smith)

The practice of compacting with a brush (Fig 239) may once have been better known. Townsend in his SPAB Information Sheet *Roughcast for Historic Buildings* has a footnote to the effect that there are renders:

> in some parts of the country (eg Berkshire, Wiltshire, Gloucestershire) which are formed by beating smooth render with a brush of twigs (to re-work the surface in order to reduce shrinkage). (SPAB 1990)

LIMEWASHING

The traditional finish to lime plasters and renders has always been limewash. As noted earlier limewash layers, mostly unpigmented, survived over all the areas of original plaster at Bowhill. The first *Specification for limewash for use at Bowhill,* applied initially to internal works, and was based on Jane Schofield's SPAB leaflet *Basic limewash* (Schofield 1994). This was developed through discussion with the craftsmen involved, building on their experience and adapted to suit areas and circumstances, eg type and porosity of substrate, weather conditions, orientation of wall. The basic practice was as follows:

Preparation

- Scoop out approx 1 pint of (lime) putty into a clean bucket and macerate with a little water into a smooth paste using a whisk or potato masher.
- Continue to slowly add more water, mixing continuously, until it is like a thin cream.
- Pour mixture through a fine kitchen sieve or muslin cloth, working through any lumps (but not using force) and discard any residue left.
- Stir in the colouring pigment, if required. Pigments should be previously dissolved in hot water at a rate of approx 1 to 2 ounces per pint of lime putty used, depending on the final colour required. The colour in the bucket will be approximately twice as intense as the end result, so it is advisable to do sample tests on a piece of watercolour or other absorbent paper. If experimenting, record quantities used.
- Dilute the mixture further, mixing thoroughly, until it is the consistency of milk. Note that it is far better to have several thin layers than a couple of thick layers of limewash.

Application

- Apply the first coat very thoroughly but thinly. Dampen down the surface to be limewashed one hour

before and again just before application and paint the surface of the render using a 5" or 6" bristle brush, as evenly as possible. Re-dampen any areas that dry out before the limewash is applied. The colour will not show (it will be transparent on application) but it is important not to go over an area already covered, even if it is tempting to do so. The colour will begin to appear after subsequent applications and drying. Subsequent coats should be applied after the previous coats have dried; overnight or 24 hours should be adequate. Apply a total of at least 5 coats, this will depend on appearance, following the same procedures for each coat. It may be advisable to make the first coat or two especially runny in order to get a better key to the render.[50]

Limewash was also applied internally direct to one or two areas of daub ie to the north elevation of the double-lath daub partition in the Hall, to both sides of the similar but haired-cob plaster, panel between Great and Inner Chambers, south range, and to the reveals of an adjacent window, also heavily-haired daub plastered. An initial trial patch on the hall panel dried too quickly into the daub, the surface cracking cuboidally. This experience reinforced the spraying up the background, runny-application, regime. As noted earlier, the ends of binding hairs had sprung-out all over the surface of the haired-cob plasters. There was much debate about how to get rid of these. In the end the mason (pers comm Charles Smith) found he could simply paint them in, stick them to the wall, with lime wash as he applied it. After the requisite number of coats, the hairs had, to all intents and purposes, been lost in the slightly grainy overall appearance of the finished work. The same limewash mix was applied over most plaster and render, new and historic, internally and externally (Figs 240 and 241).

Figure 240 Finishes to render, Mark Joy limewashing new render over composite wall areas of stone and cob, East elevation, Great Hall, 1993.

Figure 241 Finishes to render, west elevation (kitchen, west gable of south range and rebuilt timber-framed and rendered mid-nineteenth-century extension) with limewash completed, 1995.

Figure 242 Finishes and presentation, original cob and blocking to vertical chase at the side of jointed-cruck post in the wall, south range. The window is not original but a later insertion. This area was initially left as an educational panel (plastered over in 1996), 1995.

Figure 243 Finishes and presentation, Oriel Chamber, detail of cob-block repair beneath end of lintel, again initially left unplastered for educational reasons (plastered over in 1996), 1996.

Tallowed limewash, the tallow intended for additional waterproofing, was used in the top three external coats to the south range west gable, the part of the fabric most exposed to bad weather. It was also used where it had previously been employed, as well as over cement renders, both cases where background suction would be too low for normal limewash to bond well (pers comm Charles Smith).

FINISHES AND PRESENTATION

The issue of the didactic, or educational, presentation of the building and the works was discussed in Chapter 2. There it was noted that many features contributing to an understanding of the fabric are inevitably concealed when finishes are applied. It was therefore decided to leave some selected areas of interior wall unplastered, subject to the needs of any user eventually found for the building. Those areas of earth wall chosen were a small section abutting a jointed cruck post, showing the way in which the *c* 1500 work had proceeded, a section of new cob cross-wall showing the character of the modern material, a small cob-block repair to the Oriel Chamber wall and the north, first floor, interior elevation of the kitchen gable. Also arranged for display was the Great Hall side of repaired double-lath daubed panel 1.

Figure 244 View of east and south elevations of building on completion of repair and reconstruction, 1995.

This was given a hinged cover for protection and so as not to disturb the architectural character of this key space.

The kitchen wall left unfinished displayed a range of matters relevant to the project, eg the original use of cob and stone, the original fitting of the jointed cruck posts to the walls, the texture and consituents of the 500-year old cob and course lift/day-work joints in that material. New and repair works displayed were stonework repointing in lime mortar, cob-block repair, mass cob/lime repair, daub dubbing-out, a small section of shuttered cob and surface repairs in punned cob alone.

One of the most rewarding aspects of the whole operation was the enthusiastic reaction of interested members of the public to these particular *in situ* repair works displays (Figs 242 and 243). (All of these were subsequently plastered over as they were unlikely to be appropriate to future users of the building.) Externally the painting of yellow ochred limewash over the whole structure, its colour and intensity changing hygroscopically with the changing weather, has produced a landmark of startling exoticism within this essentially suburban part of Exeter (Fig 244).

7   Conclusion

The first aim of works of conservation must be to repair fabric considered to be worthy of preservation using as appropriate, either the original, or more modern, technology. Following on from this, restoration seeks to put back known but missing fabric to match in form and material that which was once there. Such fabric may be fully or only partly recreated. The philosophical background to decisions relating to these fundamental matters has been considered elsewhere (Harrison 1996, 14-29).

That judgements have been made at Bowhill is implied in every case that has been examined. The strategic dilemmas raised are common to all works involving any element of conservation and their outcomes are embodied in the repaired and reinstated building. As far as the cob and daub works go, the end results to date, in terms of function and appearance, seem satisfactory. The same can be said for the new interior plaster and exterior render over stone and cob.[51]

Sometimes circumstances meant that intentions could not be fulfilled, hence the use of cob-blocks in the cob cross- and kitchen walls. Here the blocks are a compromise but remain far and away a better solution than would brick or concrete block. Long-term relationships between cob and oak were there to be seen in the building; how more modern materials interreact with cob over long periods of time is less certain.

The remaining, subsidiary, aims at Bowhill related to the opportunity the works offered for the examination and use of earthen materials, and the subsequent dissemination of information on what had been learned about them. The site processes gave both management and works staff the chance to develop their understanding of, and skills in using, cob and daub. The practical activity shown in the photo-record is confirmation of the confidence in the use of the materials that developed over the 5-year period of the second stage works, at all levels within the project team. The views of all concerned were respected and taken into account as the exploration of the potential and limits of the materials went on. The practical observations of the skilled labourers and craftsmen, who, in the end, make any job, were balanced by, and joined to, the analytical approach of the site agent, engineer, directing architectural staff and Inspector, to produce the results documented here. Interactive discussion was deliberately extended to a number of sessions with slides of work in progress analysed by the whole team to arrive at joint conclusions on the nature and performance of the material.

At the outset a strategic commitment was made to treat the works as a test-bed, to learn from mistakes as well as from successes. The intention, stated at the inaugural meeting of DEBA, was to use Bowhill as an exemplar in order to raise levels of perception about the versatility of cob and, particularly, to demonstrate that repairs to it and to daub can be managed in a practical way. One important lesson to be learned here relates to the planned management of the material, more especially its preparation. Had serious subsoil sampling and mix balancing taken place, then some of the difficulties arising from shrinkage would not have developed. Simple tests can be made and always should be. The bibliography lists some sources of advice.

A key component of the project was the photo-record. The illustrations in this study are a selection from a much more extensive collection, both in black and white and in colour slides, all taken on request by David Garner for English Heritage. These now form a resource deposited in the English Heritage Photo Library. Considerable attention was given between 1990 and 1995 to ensuring that photography was focused on those issues most germane to this report.

Similarly, time had to be found for observation, discussion and feed-back, especially, as noted above, with the craftsmen, to ensure that a coherent, useful works record was made as the five years ran their course.

The combination of these last two record programmes has allowed the achievement of the major secondary project, the dissemination here of experience gained at Bowhill. It is hoped that at least some of those drawn to the subject will have found something useful or stimulating here and that they may be encouraged to take things further.

Bibliography

Addey S O, 1933 *The Evolution of the English House,* 2nd edn, London, Allen & Unwin.

Andrews W P, 1955 *Soil Cement Roads,* 3rd revised edn, London, Cement & Concrete Association.

Allen C B, 1849–50 *Cottage Building, or, Hints for Improving the Dwellings of the Labouring Classes,* London, John Weale.

anon, 1918 The revival of cob cottages in Devon, *Country Life,* **43**, 22 June, 567–9.

Ashurst J and Ashurst N, 1988a *Brick, Terracotta and Earth,* English Heritage Technical Handbook **2**: Practical Building Conservation, Aldershot, Gower Press.

Ashurst J and Ashurst N, 1988b *Mortars, Plasters and Renders,* English Heritage Technical Handbook **3**: Practical Building Conservation, Aldershot, Gower Press.

Arkell W J and Tomkieff S I, 1953 *English Rock Terms,* Oxford, Oxford University Press.

Beacham P (ed), 1990 *Devon Building, an Introduction to Local Traditions,* Exeter, Devon Books.

Bedford P, Induni B, Induni L and Keefe L, 1993 *Appropriate Plasters, Renders and Finishes for Cob and Random Stone Walls in Devon,* Exeter, Devon Earth Building Association.

Best H, 1857 *Rural Economy in Yorkshire in 1641, being the Farming and Account Books of Henry Best,* Durham, Surtees Society .

Blaylock S R, forthcoming *Bowhill, Exeter,* Exeter, Exeter Archaeology.

Brady N C, 1974 *The Nature and Properties of Soils,* 8th edn, London, Macmillan.

Brereton C, 1991 *The Repair of Historic Buildings: Advice on Principles and Method,* London, English Heritage.

British Standards Institution, 1984 *BS6100 British Standard Glossary of Building and Civil Engineering terms, Part 6,* Watford, British Standards Institution.

Brunskill R W, 1970 *Illustrated Handbook of Vernacular Architecture,* London, Faber & Faber.

Brunskill R W, 1985 *Timber Building in Britain,* London, Gollancz.

Caroe A D R and Caroe M B, 1984 *Stonework: Maintenance and Surface Repair,* London, CIO Publishing.

Charles F W B, 1990 *Conservation of Timber Buildings,* London, Stanley Thornes.

Cleghorn W H (ed), 1979 *Stabilised Soil, An Under-used Resource for Low-cost Building in Developing Countries,* Glasgow, University of Strathclyde.

Coke T, Findlay D, Halsey R and Williamson E, 1982 *Recording a Church: An Illustrated Glossary,* London, Council for British Archaeology.

Collyns W, 1857, in *Notes and Queries,* **4**:91, 258.

Cox J, 1996 Georgian mud and straw in Devon and Cornwall, in *Georgian Vernacular: Papers given at a Georgian Group Symposium, 28 October 1995,* (ed) Burton N, London, 19–26.

Crocker A, 1804 On cottages, *The Husbandry and Internal Improvement of the Country,* Commissioners to the Board of Agriculture, part **XI**, 2nd ed, Frome.

Curl J, 1996 *An Encyclopaedia of Architectural Terms,* Shaftesbury, Donhead Publishing.

Devon Historic Buildings Trust Technical Panel, 1992a *The Cob Buildings of Devon, 1: History, Building Methods & Conservation,* Exeter, Devon Historic Buildings Trust.

Devon Historic Buildings Trust Technical Panel, 1992b *The Cob Buildings of Devon, 2: Decay, Structural Failure and Repair,* Exeter, Devon Historic Buildings Trust.

Dibben J C, 1914 letter, *Country Life,* **35**, 4th April, 502–3.

Doat P, Hays A, Houben H, Matuk S and Vitoux F, 1979 *Construire en Terre,* Grenoble, Craterre.

Dobson E, 1850 (1971) A rudimentary treatise on the manufacture of bricks and tiles, *Journal of Ceramic History,* **5**.

Duncan R, 1947 *Home Made Home,* London, Faber.

English Heritage, 1997 *Hybrid Mortar Mixes,* technical policy statement, London, English Heritage.

Fenton A and Walker B, 1981 *The Rural Architecture of Scotland,* Edinburgh, John Donald.

Greer M J A, 1996 *The Effect of Moisture Content and Composition on the Compressive Strength and Rigidity of Cob Made from Soil of the Breccia Measures near Teignmouth, Devon,* unpublished M Phil thesis, University of Plymouth.

Gwilt J, 1867 [1982] *The Encyclopaedia of Architecture,* New York, Crown Publishers Inc..

Hamer F and Hamer J, 1977 *Clays,* London, Pitman.

Hardy T, 1888 (1930), Fellow Townsmen, in *Wessex Tales,* London, Macmillan, 111–178.

Harman, 1929 *Buckinghamshire Dialect* (ed G Eland), London, Hazell, Watson and Viney.

Harrison J R, 1984 The mud wall in England at the close of the vernacular era, in *Transactions of the Ancient Monuments Society,* ns **28**, 154–74.

Harrison J R, 1989 Some clay dabbins in Cumberland: their construction and form. Part 1, in *Transactions of the Ancient Monuments Society,* ns **33**, 97–151.

Harrison J R, 1991 Some clay dabbins in Cumberland: their construction and form. Part 2, in *Transactions of the Ancient Monuments Society,* ns **35**, 29–88.

Harrison J R, 1996 Changing perceptions of architectural-historic value, a case study: Bowhill, Devon, in *ASCHB Transactions,* **20**, 14–29.

Hill, The Rev. C, 1843 On the construction of cottages, *Journal of the Royal Agricultural Society,* 356–69.

Holmes S and Wingate M, 1997 *Building with Lime,* London, Intermediate Technology Publications.

Hoskins W G, 1973 *English Landscapes,* London, BBC.

Hughes R, 1982 Material and structural behaviour of soil-constructed walls, *Monumentum,* **26**:3, 176–86.

Hutchinson P O, 1890 letter, *The Western Antiquary,* **10**, 166–7.

Innocent C F, 1916 [1971] *The Development of English Building Construction,* Newton Abbot, David & Charles.

Jaggard W R, 1922 *Experimental Cottages, A Report of the Work of the Department at Amesbury, Wilts,* London, HMSO.

Jaggard W R and Drury F E, 1949–51 *Architectural Building Construction,* 3 vols, Cambridge, Cambridge University Press.

James J F, 1977 Vernacular architecture in the New Forest, *Hampshire Field Club, New Forest Section, Annual Report,* 20–25.

Johnson S W, 1806 *Rural Economy containing a Treatise on Pisé Building etc,* New York, Riley (1979 Ann Arbor, University Microfilms).

Keefe L N, 1998, *An Investigation into the Cause of Structural Failure in Traditional Cob Buildings*, unpublished MPhil thesis, University of Plymouth.

Law H, 1855 *Rudiments of the Art of Constructing and Repairing Common Roads*, London, John Weale.

Laycock C H, 1920 The old Devon farmhouse, Part I, *Transactions of the Devonshire Association*, **52**, 158–91.

Long J D, 1929 *Adobe Construction*, UCLA Bulletin **427**, Berkeley, Ca, UCLA.

Loudon J C, 1836 *Encyclopaedia of Cottage, Farm and Villa Architecture*, London, Longman, Rees, Orme, Brown, Green & Longman.

Marshall W, 1796 (1970) *Marshall's Rural Economy of the West of England*, **1**, Newton Abbot, David & Charles.

McCann J, 1995 *Clay & Cob Buildings*, 2nd edn, Princes Risborough, Shire.

McGregor C and Walker B, 1996 *Earth Structures and Construction in Scotland*, Historic Scotland Technical Advice Note **6,** Edinburgh, Historic Scotland.

McLean J and Scott J, 1993 *The Penguin Dictionary of Building*, 4th edn, London, Penguin.

Merion-Jones G I, 1982 *The Vernacular Architecture of Brittany*, Edinburgh, John Donald.

Mullins L C (ed), 1940 (1987) *The Architectural Treasures of Early America; vol 1; Survey of Early American Design*, Harrisburg, Pa, The National Historical Society.

Neve, 1726 (1969) *The City and Country Purchaser and Builder's Dictionary: The Compleat Builder's Guide*, Newton Abbot, David & Charles.

Norton J, 1986 (1997) *Building with Earth, A Handbook*, Intermediate Technology Group, Rugby.

Oliver B W, 1949 The Devonshire cottage, *Report and Transactions of the Devonshire Association*, **81**, 28–44.

Oxford English Reference Dictionary, 1995 J Pearson & B Trumble (eds), Oxford, Oxford University Press.

Pannell J P M, 1964 (1977) *Man the Builder: An Illustrated History of Engineering*, London, Thames and Hudson.

Parker S P (ed), 1997 *McGraw Hill Dictionary of Geology and Mineralogy*, New York, McGraw Hill.

Pearson G T, 1992 *Conservation of Clay & Chalk Buildings*, London, Donhead.

Powys A R, 1929 (1995) *Repair of Ancient Buildings*, London, SPAB.

Price C A, 1984 The consolidation of limestone using a poultice and limewater, in *Adhesives and Consolidants*, London, International Institute for Conservation, 160–2.

Price C A and Ross K D, 1984 The cleaning and treatment of limestone by the lime method, part I: a technical appraisal of stone conservation techniques employed at Wells Cathedral, *Momentum*, **Winter**, 301–12.

Risdon T, 1785 (1970) *A Review of part of Risdon's Survey of Devon containing the general description of that County; with corrections, annotations and additions. By the late William Chapple of Exeter*, Barnstaple, Porcupine.

Rose W, 1937 (1987) *The Village Carpenter*, London, Black.

Salzman L F, 1952 (1992) *Building in England down to 1540*, Oxford, Oxford University Press.

Schofield J, 1985 (1994) *Basic Limewash*, SPAB Information Sheet **IN/1**, London, SPAB.

Taylor R F, 1966 *Three cruck buildings in Lancashire and Cheshire – 1, Pudding Pie Nook, Wrea Green*, Historical Society of Lancashire and Cheshire, **117**, 33–47.

Thompson M W, 1981 *Ruins, Their Preservation & Display*, London, British Museum Publications Ltd.

Torr C, 1921 *Small Talk at Wreyland*, Cambridge, Cambridge University Press.

Townsend A, 1989, 1990 *Rough Cast for Historic Buildings*, SPAB Information Sheet **IN/11**, London, SPAB.

Teutonico J (ed), 1997 *The English Heritage Directory of Building Limes*, Shaftesbury, Donhead Publishing.

Walker B, 1977 *Clay buildings in North-east Scotland*, Dundee, Scottish Vernacular Buildings Working Group.

Watson L and Harris R, 1994–5 Out of earth 1 & 2, in *Proceedings of the Earthen Architecture Conferences held at the Centre for Earthen Architecture, Plymouth School of Architecture*, Plymouth, University of Plymouth.

Watson R C and McClintock M E, 1979 *Traditional Houses of the Fylde*, Centre for North-West Regional Studies Occasional Paper **6,** Lancaster, University of Lancaster.

Williams-Ellis C, 1919–20 (1947) *Building in Cob, Pisé, Chalk and Clay*, ed Williams-Ellis C and Eastwick Field J, London, Country Life.

Wood J, 1806 (1972) *A Series of Plans for Cottages or Habitations of the Labourer etc*, Farnborough, Gregg Reprints.

Endnotes

1 Information here about Bowhill's history and development is drawn from Exeter Archaeology's *Bowhill, Exeter* Archive Reports produced under the direction of Stuart Blaylock and whose monograph report is forthcoming. A number of drawings are based on the Archive Reports' excellent record drawings and where this is so Exeter Archaeology is credited.

2 An example is found at Gurney Street Manor, Cannington, Somerset, where the pentice is a freestanding structure crossing a courtyard from Hall to Kitchen.

3 Bowhill is a listed building and as such it is by law afforded a degree of protection from arbitrary change. Protection, and, following on from this, preservation, may be justified because of the particular aesthetic and stylistic qualities of a structure, its 'intrinsic merit', or its rarity. A building may also be considered an irreplaceable 'document' in its own right, demonstrating past aspirations, past socio-economic conditions, past techniques – in other words it may be 'material evidence' of former ways of life and ways of doing things, on a par with an object in a museum. This latter, didactic – educational – imperative in fact became an important contributory reason for the state to 'take buildings into care' (into 'Guardianship') – as exemplars, as typical or special examples of their kind. Bowhill fell within this category.

4 For more than 100 years, from 1882, the state has identified certain very important historic buildings and sites, giving them statutory protection from alteration and damage as Scheduled Ancient Monuments. Most remain in private hands. The government manages some four hundred indirectly through English Heritage; only a few are actually owned by the state or English Heritage. Power to take individual privately-owned Scheduled Ancient Monuments and, more recently, Listed Buildings into Guardianship and to manage them for their owners was given to the Office of Works in 1900. In 1910 it was also enabled to accept them as outright gifts. English Heritage and its predecessors, (including the Ministry of Works and the Department of the Environment) have been delegated responsibility for managing Guardianship properties by the Secretary of State.

Only a limited number of properties (approximately 400) are in state care or Guardianship. Nonetheless these consist of a wide and very important selection of structures, earthworks and – predominantly – ruins. Up until recently the general aim was to repair and to then turn such sites and buildings into 'custodial' sites, sites employing permanent custodians, open to the public in perpetuity for educational purposes. Roofed buildings were rarely taken into Guardianship except as an act of last resort, when, for instance, their survival was threatened. This was one aspect of the case with Bowhill which was acquired in 1976. Bowhill is a Grade I Listed Building rather than a Scheduled Ancient Monument. Today, nationally, Listed Buildings vastly outnumber Scheduled Ancient Monuments. Listing, which came into operation after the Second World War under the Ministry of Housing and Local Government, includes occupied buildings; Scheduled buildings and sites are usually unoccupied and often roofless.

5 Inspectors of Ancient Monuments and Historic Buildings form part of the staff of English Heritage. They provide expert advice to English Heritage, local authorities and central government. The Inspectorate developed initially to advise on the identification of Britain's historic built heritage assets and then, with architects, engineers and surveyors, to set patterns for their repair and preservation. Their primary contribution has always been academic, providing central and local government with authoritative and impartial justification for the preservation and interpretation of historic buildings and ancient monuments. Inspectors, whether from an archaeological or an art-historical background, work as applied historians on the buildings and sites on which they advise. Their advice is sought in the selection, grant-aid and statutory control of ancient monuments, Listed Buildings and Conservation Areas. Their job is to unravel the history and structural development of these sites and monuments and to place them in their artistic, archaeological and environmental context and to identify the 'heritage' significance of their different elements.

6 Under the old DEL system, at each monthly site visit a record of management decisions was made by the site chargehand. This was approved by management and was then known as the Visiting Officers' Report (VOR). These lasted in use, in concert with monthly reports, until 1983. They formed the instruction for the next phase of the works. In the heyday of the system, between the 1930s and 1950s, they were supplemented by meticulous drawings provided by the then Ancients Monuments Drawing Office to show new construction, complex timber repairs etc. Where these included survey drawings they are second to none in terms of quality, information and layout. Works of general monument repair and fabric consolidation were not, however, normally detailed or recorded; the argument was that the result was its own record.

Given the relatively limited range of operations involved in much monument maintenance and repair, particularly with the ruins which make up the bulk of the Historic Properties (as sites in English Heritage care are currently known), the DEL system worked satisfactorily for many years. It cannot however be said to have been foolproof and, as with any other similar organisation, it was at times open to abuse.

From 1983 a system of individual requisitions from management, falling somewhere between that described above and more usual commercial practice, effectively Architect's Instructions, was instituted. The story came full circle in 1996 when complete privatization saw the end of the special relationship.

7 Extract from *A short talk on the repair of cob buildings*, given to the Society for the Protection of Ancient Buildings by Rex Gardiner in the 1960s or '70s.

8 Historians of the man-made English and Welsh landscapes have conventionally divided the country into highland and lowland areas. The frontier is roughly an imaginary line drawn across the map from the Tees in the north-east to the Exe in the south-west. (Hoskins 1973, 7). To the west of the line

lie the highland, and to the east the lowland zones. Hoskins notes that this view is 'full of contradictions' but it retains its general validity.

9 In many of the earlier and also for the most basic examples of the system the jointed cruck wall-posts terminate near ground level. (Bowhill is of course an exception, numbers of its jointed crucks being reared on storey height stone walls.) By the eighteenth and nineteenth centuries in Devon the wall-posts had disappeared leaving truss couples supported by mass stone or mud walls. Though the use of the cruck seems to have been endemic with cob, there is no practical reason why in the past mud could not have been combined with the box frame in a similar way, as was demonstrated by the success of repairs at Bowhill with its wall top eaves-purlins (wall-plates) in place before mud-work repair below was added.

10 Sometimes, and for whatever reason, local timber-frame building tradition did not allow for the usual more or less substantial intermediate studs found in the thin daubed walls of south-eastern and Midland England. The resulting wide panels, lacking the rigidity given by the studs between main posts, had to carry a thicker coat of daub in order to stiffen the wall. Typical internal reinforcement to such panels takes the form of vertically set rods, split or whole, or, in the better work, riven-oak lath. These span between the sole- and wall-plate, the buildings in question being of one or at the most one and a half storeys. In some cases, a horizontal mid-rail halves the span of the rods and the daub thickness can be reduced again. In some houses on the Lancastrian Fylde plain, the vertical rods, here split-laths known locally as 'clam-staffs' (ie 'clay' staffs) are fixed so far apart that panel thickness comes near to that of normal, unreinforced mud walling. For further information, see John Summerson's drawings in Addey 1933, Watson & McClintock 1979 and Taylor 1966. Personal information from R Taylor of RCHME.

11   having generally a footing of stone wall two foot high, on which is placed a strong cill of timber: to which is superadded uprights of quartering, two feet apart, into which are inserted rounds of rough wood, like ladder work, at six or seven inches one above the other ... [the] ... spaces ... between ... [being] ... well filled with a mixture of mire [mud/daub] and long straw, previously well trodden together, provincially called cab-dab. (Crocker 1804)

The whole was then recommended for plastering and 'rough-casting'. Similar arrangements are found in some other parts of England as well as near at hand across the Channel in Normandy and Picardy. Studs may be exposed or plastered over. Information relating to Kent from M O'Connor RIBA and to Picardy, F Kelly.

12 Loudon, writing in 1836, may be speaking of it when he notes:

Instead of brick nogging for partitions, cob is used for filling in the framework, which is previously lathed with slit oak or hazel. This sort of work is called rab and dab (Loudon 1836, 417).

A version recorded in the eastern USA is described thus:

In New England we have the very early custom of placing the original split oak clapboards directly upon the exterior uprights of the old oak frames ... the wall facing of the room inside being then either plastered on split laths ... nailed to the inner face of the frame, or sometimes faced on the interior with wide horizontal pine boarding, with feather edge or

lapped joints. An instance of a dwelling, built in 1649, illustrates the former method ... the space between the studs was filled with puddled clay, probably from the inside as the split lath boards were added course over course. The clay was fluid enough to work out and fill up the spaces between the lapping oak rived clapboards, which were probably also plugged up with moist clay from the exterior, to insulate the wall and keep it tight against weather and cold (Mullins 1987, 211).

The term 'double lath' is adopted here throughout as a convenient shorthand description of the system. It is not to be confused with nineteenth-century building terminology in which laths for plastering are, according to their thickness, called 'single, something less than a quarter of an inch, lath-and-a-half and double. The first is the thinnest ... the second is about one-third thicker ... and the double lath is twice the thickness' (Gwilt 1867, 675). This differentiation and nomenclature continued on, being repeated in Jaggard & Drury, **2**, 375, in the mid twentieth century.

13 Alfred Howard is many different things, ex-Royal Engineer, a fount of the Devon vernacular and the oral tradition of the rural building trade, a wonderful handler of oak, a brilliant observer and technical improviser, a man entirely at home with the practicalities of modern building.

14 This activity and growth in awareness has been parallelled by similar developments in other parts of Britain. Local groups have been formed in East Anglia (EARTHA), the East Midlands (EMESS) and Harborough & Daventry (HADES) for example. An understanding of the nature and performance of chalk-cob has been developing since the early 1980s in Hampshire, thanks largely to the efforts of Gordon Pearson. A Centre for Earthern Architecture has recently been established at the University of Plymouth while the wider national interests have been brought together under the umbrella of the ICOMOS UK Earth Structures Committee. This grouping includes delegates from Scotland and Wales as well as England. Finally there are now even some signs that earth may become architecturally chic. The well-known architectural practice Fielden Clegg is building an 'Earth Centre exhibition complex' (with Millennium funds), at Doncaster. The front wall of this is to be built in 'earth'.

15 Notably Larry Keefe, staff and students at the Departments of Architecture and Materials Science, the University of Plymouth. See also Greer 1996.

16 Tests carried out on cob blocks in relation to M J A Greer's thesis at the University of Plymouth proved this point, 1995–6.

17 Hardy, in one of his short stories ('Fellow Townsmen' in *Wessex Tales*) set in the middle of the nineteenth century, refers to the care that was sometimes formerly taken with brickwork, especially with foundations.

A building in an old fashioned town five and thirty years ago did not, as in the modern fashion, rise from the sod like a booth at a fair. The foundations and lower courses were put in and allowed to settle for many weeks before the super-structure was built up, and a whole summer of drying was hardly sufficient to do justice to the important issues involved.

By contrast Salzman reproduces a contract for the building of a mud structure in Exeter in 1478, almost contemporary with the building of Bowhill. He notes that it is an

Agreement by a mason to build a malthouse, 20 ft by 14 ft of two storeys, with mud walls on stone sleeper walls and a roof of 3 crucks (Salzman 1952, 540).

The work was to start at the end of April and be completed by Michaelmas, some six months. The building was to have ten-foot (3m) high mud side-walls over a two-foot (0.6m) high stone plinth. It appears that its (specified) first floor must have been loaded onto the new cob. For the whole to be completed in this time indicates just how confident in their ability to manage cob the medieval builders were, especially when one considers that the interiors of their mud walls were probably still not dry a year later. This is confidence which may be beginning to return. In the summer of 1993, builder Kevin McCabe, working over a three-month period, put up new cob walling in a barn conversion near Honiton nine (2.7m) to ten (3m) foot high in the side walls and 15 (4.5m) to 16 (4.8m) foot high in the gable. The material, improved by mixing with sand, was laid wetter than is usual and initial shrinkage downward in a three foot high 'lift' was as much as two inches. The lower lifts support heavy first-floor beams in places.

In summer 1997 a very large group of volunteers, directed by Bob Bennett and Trevor Innes built and roofed a mud cottage on a site in the New Forest, in one day. The floor area was 30 square metres. The walls were two feet (0.6m) thick and about six feet (1.8m) high, and required some 44 tonnes of 'clay' (from *Building Engineer*, October 1997, 22–4).

18 This comment on the nature of the local subsoil is taken from a summary by Larry Keefe.

19 Research undertaken as part of an M Phil project by Larry Keefe at the University of Plymouth.

20 The advice note of John Ashurst, then Senior Ancient Monuments Architect, to the then Superintendent of Works at Bowhill recommends 'stablised earth construction, using the pisé de terre technique of ramming a semi-wet mix between shutter boards', the material being short straw and subsoil from the site mixed 3:1 with 'fresh dry hydraulic lime'. The new cob was to be internally secured at intervals to any existing cob, using 'galvanised brick reinforcement'.

21 From the diary of the July 1971 student work party at Sheldon Farm, Dunsford, near Exeter, Devon (Anon), directed by John Deal ARIBA with the assistance of Alan Thomas RIBA. Information from John Deal ARIBA. To 'puddle' is to prepare 'puddled clay', the material traditionally used to waterproof the beds of reservoirs, canals, etc. '...the clay is mixed with a preparation of sand, wetted and kneaded, it becomes a completely leakproof lining and remains so as long as it is kept in the wetted condition. The kneading of the plastic clay was performed either by labourers who "heeled" it with their boots, or by animals driven over the surface until the right quality of puddle was achieved,' Pannell (1964) 1977, 60.

22 'Clat' was apparently a Devon term; see Laycock 1920, 179 and 187, for 'clat, a clod or ball of earth'.

23 For traditional cob construction in the New Forest see James 1977. Alfred Howard's definition of shillet is small fractured stone and subsoil lying directly over the bedrock. B W Oliver notes 'Where possible a good clay with a large content of small shillet stone was selected, or small flat stones might be added (Oliver 1949, 37). Arkell & Tomkieff define shillet as 'the shales of the Culm Measures in Devon and Somerset ... A dialect word from the same root as SHALE. Immediate

derivation from ME verb "sheel" (15th century), shell, shale or shill, meaning "shell off", "decorticate"'(Arkell & Tomkieff 1953, 106).

There are a number of good early nineteenth century and later references to the type of material best suited to mud-wall building. Johnson clearly knew Devon very well indeed. He notes that soils unsuitable for cob are those with the 'lightness of poor lands' and the 'tenacity of strong clay' and mentions that brick-earths may be used,

> but these, if they are used alone, are apt to crack, owing to their tenacity of moisture: however, persons who understand the business and can shade them in drying, will use them to good purpose ... [also acceptable are] ... strong earths with a mixture of small gravel, which are refused by the brick makers and potters. These gravelly earths are very useful, the best pisé is made of them (Johnson 1806, 41).

For Johnson the signs of potential cob-making material in the field are when the spade produces:

> large lumps of earth at a time ... when arable land lies in clods or large lumps and binds after a heavy shower and a hot sun; when field-mice have made themselves subterranean passages ... and these are clear and smooth ... When roads, having been worn away ... are lower than the other lands, and the sides of the road support themselves almost upright ... wherever there are deep ruts, and when dry very difficult to turn the wheels out of them, there is certainly an abundance of soil fit for the purpose (op cit, 42).

Johnson also recommends the mixing of soils for better performance, a practice which has been employed in England at different times. Some of his topographical indicators of suitable soil will be very familiar to those who know the Devon countryside.

24 See Merion-Jones 1982; pages 48–50 summarize the method of managing relatively liquid material placed between shutters. There seems to have been a considerable variety of technique employed in Brittany.

25 In summertime we usually fetch clottes out of the field to make mortar on, but in winter we either schoole up some dirte together ... or otherwise wee digge downe some olde clay or mudde-wall (Best 1857, 145).

26 For instance, in Wales, the record tells us, cob was sometimes mixed in shallow pits, where it would no doubt have been heavily watered, and then animals were driven through it. In the New Forest after mixing, the cob was sometimes run to a slurry and then left to drain before use. In south-west Scotland in 1810 it was reported that before mixing builders worked 'common clay' into 'good mortar' and let this stand 'to get more consistency' (letter to the Earl of Mansfield concerning his Annandale Estates, Mansfield Muniments, NRA [S] 0776). Information from B. Walker.

There is a cross-over with conventional brick-making practice. Gwilt (1867, Book II, 524) notes in relation to the preparation of brick-earths:

This branch of the manufacture was formerly executed by throwing the clay into shallow pits and subjecting it to be trodden by men and oxen ... [the method] has been advantageously superseded by a clay- or pug-mill, with a horse track.

Edward Dobson, writing in 1850, discusses hand-mixing material for burnt bricks under 'tempering'.

The object of tempering is to bring the prepared brick earth into a homogenous paste, for the use of the moulder.

The old-fashioned way of tempering was to turn the clay over repeatedly with shovels, and to tread it over by horses and men, until it acquired the requisite plasticity. This method is still practiced in many country yards. (Dobson 1971, **1**, 24)

27 Extract from a lecture, *A Short Talk on the Repair of Cob Buildings,* given to the Society for the Protection of Ancient Buildings by Rex Gardiner in the 1960s/70s; 'most of the cobs were wet mixed with chopped straw or cat flights which made it easier to handle'.

28 An early suggestion that fibre might also distribute shrinkage as the cob dried appears in Duncan 1947, 124 where it is noted 'My own theory ... is that the straw, on being easily compressed, takes up any shrinkage in the wall and distributes it about the mass of the wall, so that no exterior cracks are caused'. Parts of this book are an excellent commentary on the subject in Devon. A similar view is given by Williams-Ellis & Eastwick Field in their 1947 revision of Clough Williams-Ellis's *Building in Cob, Pisé and Stabilised Earth.*

Tests in California in 1929 with unconsolidated 'poured adobe' or 'mud concrete' as it was termed, showed that:

> With many soils, as the walls dry out vertical cracks will develop ... Unless these are continuous through a considerable height of wall or of a width greater than one sixteenth of an inch, they do not appear to weaken the wall materially ... Mixing straw with the soil lessens the tendency to cracking ... There appear to be two beneficial results from mixing straw with earth ... In wet mixes the straw apparently serves as drainage channels, assisting in conducting the moisture from the centre of the mass as it dries. It has been observed that some soils shrink and crack less ... if straw is added to the mix. And in one series of tests using one soil type in the rammed earth method (pisé) the straw proved a reinforcement, increasing the compressive strength [by] nearly 80%. Straw in lengths of two to six inches is easier to incorporate in the mixture than the long length. (Long 1929, 9, 26)

29 Personal communication with John Uglow, Thoverton, Devon in 1980. He had noted blocks in four buildings in the village. Those used internally at one cottage measured $14^1/_4$" x 6" x 4" (362 x 150 x 100mm).

30 With the conjunction of clay and chalk in the mix we arrive at a variety of mud wall still much in evidence in southern counties such as Hampshire and, in the block, and also mass, form, parts of East Anglia. This is immediately recognisable by its white, cream or greyish colour.

31 Something like a 'trestle piece' occurs under the end of one jointed-cruck-leg extended right down to the top of the stone ground-floor plinth. In fact this is more likely to be a precaution against rising damp. Loudon notes 'The lintels ... are put in as the work advances (allowance being made for settling), bedding them on cross pieces (1836, 39).

32 There remains controversy as to whether or not the door opening was an original feature.

33 Carefully carried out, and using mist sprays, no difficulty was experienced with thoroughly wetting-up historic cob at Bowhill. Spraying should cease when the wall face begins to erode materially but may start again when the cob is seen to have soaked up the surplus water (which happened almost immediately at Bowhill).

34 (Williams-Ellis 1919 [1947], 39.) This instrument, in association with cob, is also mentioned by Loudon (1836, 47): 'It is usual to pare down the side of each sucessive rise before another is added to it. The instrument used for this purpose is like a baker's peel ... but the cob parer is made of iron'. Some descriptions of cob building suggest that paring was not done until the wall was complete. A disadvantage of this approach can be significant hardening of the lower wall courses. This can make the job extremely tiring and calls for skill in keeping the wall face true as course is piled on course.

35 A few years ago it was said that similar 'boxes' occasionally come to light at country auctions. It is likely that the benefits of heavy shuttering, theoretically no need for paring back, good potential compression, have always been known. Lightweight shuttering in the form of wattled panelling, presumably on a support system of some sort, was certainly used in the last century in the New Forest and Devon. Such shutters would surely not have allowed very serious beating of the cob. (Information from J Morgan and J Vicary, Devon and J James, New Forest, Hampshire.) Latterly, shuttering seems to have been quite well used in Devon although Alfred Howard had heard nothing of it.

36 By contrast, within the kitchen the building's jointed-crucks had been 'raised' into position before the cob was built. (The hole in the base of one of the cruck-posts which was used to facilitate moving and adjusting the cruck into position, a feature of the cruck construction system nationally, was still visible.) This was evident from the existence of a vertical shrinkage gap in the east wall cob, about 1" (25mm) wide, away from the side of the cruck-post. This degree of unattended horizontal shrinkage confirms that the builders were confident it was not a problem; it had not proved structurally deleterious. The walling here had been put up using the traditional deep course system and initial downward shrinkage was also visible within the same gap. A slight feature in the post was reverse-moulded into the cob a little below its actual location. (This revealing evidence was noticed by Rebecca Child and Francis Kelly of English Heritage.)

37 Beam-fill:
> [1842] Beam-filling. The brickwork or masonry brought up from the level of the under to the upper sides of the beams. It is also used to denote the filling up of the space from the top of the wall-plate between the rafters, to the underside of the slating, board or other covering (Gwilt 1867, 1156)

Neve (1734, 33) comments:
> Beam-filling ... Is Plaifterer's Work, 'tis only filling up the vacant Space betwixt the Raifon and the Roof, ... 'Tis a fort of Work that is very cuftomary in the Country, ... They take fome pieces of Stones, or elfe Bricks, and lay them betwixt the rafters upon the Raifon, and then Plafter upon it with Loam, or elfe they fet fome Tiles, with one edge upon the Raifon, and the other leans againft the Roof.

38 Maybe this particular rough work was done by other trades, after the masons had left the site at Leigh Barton. The problem of the sub-contractor is doubtless nothing new. Certainly filling the void with cob would have been much easier and would have resulted in a more workmanlike job than the mud-mortared rubble stone arrangement shown here.

39 John Wood speaks of 'mud' and lime thus,

I have seen those kind of walls, particularly in Cornwall, very strong and good; but if the builders would, as they lay on wet dirt, straw and small stones, throw in a small quantity of quick lime finely pounded, it would greatly strengthen the work (Wood 1806 [1972], 10).

40 John Wood's views are entirely in line with the results of modern investigations of the subject. Some tests have indicated there is an optimum lime dosage for a soil beyond which compressive strength decreases. Likely dosages are between 3% and 10% lime by dry weight, and will increase as the clay content increases (Norton 1986, 55).

the treatment of clay soils with lime ... brings an immediate reduction in plasticity and gain in strength ... In this connection, it should be noted that quicklime offers ... advantages over slaked (hydrated) lime: it dries the soil, and weight for weight is more effective ... Carbonation during curing of lime-soil mixtures is accompanied ... not only by natural drying shrinkage but by a counteracting expansion, with the result that drying shrinkage can be reduced to nearly half the normal level, with a lower resultant porosity in the dried material (Cleghorn 1979, 44).
lime may be used as a flocculating agent to break up cohesive soils and so assist the mixing process ... The use of 2% lime will overcome the acidity of soils, and will assist in stabilising acidic clays, since these soils are most susceptible to shrinkage. Sodium clays require higher proportions of lime in order to convert them to calcium clays that can be stabilised (Andrews 1955, 19).

41 Apart from savings in loadings this was, he argued, to cover the possibility that heavy furniture might be pushed against the inside wall face, so buckling it.

42 The fixing of such 'independent' structural support for heavy cementicious renders has been absolutely standard practice with mud walls in Britain since the last war. There was a large accumulation of cob-dust behind the metal lathing. This was probably the result of the initial wetting down of the wall and subsequent drying out and loss of cohesion of the cob, when the hard render was applied (pers comm Charles Smith). It indicated an extensive lack of bond between wall covering and wall, as well as the existence of a void between the two. Unfortunately, again because of time pressures, a considerable area of existing render of this type had to be left in place on part of the east wall and the north gable of the kitchen block.

43 The method involves liquid lime-putty, HTI powder (HTI is the abbreviation for high-temperature insulation or refractory brick powder insulation; when ground up it can be used as a pozzolanic additive to encourage set), water, acrylic emulsion to help adherence and sodium gluconate solution to improve fluidity. For full details of this and similar approaches to plaster consolidation see Ashurst & Ashurst 1988b, 49–85. The process as carried out at Bowhill was as follows:

• blow off loose dust etc, commence working upwards.
• using a veterinary syringe, pass a water/alcohol solution into the voids in the material. The daub absorbed a greater amount of water than an equivalent area of plaster. Saturation should, however, be avoided; work was confined to small areas at a time for this reason (say 9" to 12" square patches). Syringing stopped when water began running out of the cracks.
• the process was then repeated, but with a dilute acrylic emulsion (to help stabilize the internal edges of the cracks)

some 2 to 3 minutes after the completion of the previous stage.
• five to ten minutes after this the lime grout itself was injected, working slowly, by stages. The grout comprised liquid lime-putty, HTI powder (to help set) and a small percentage of fluidifier (sodium gluconate) to help it flow easily. To stop the grout simply flowing out again holes were plugged with cotton wool as the operation went on. (This can be seen in the photo-record). A small amount of grout penetrated right through the daub showing that some failures were continuous.
• larger surface cracks and voids were plugged using a small metal tube into which grout was poured.
• no pressing back of the original material took place.
• some grout had been allowed to run and set externally; this had a slightly disfiguring effect on the completed work.

44 Attempts to find a suitable hair for plaster mortar at Bowhill illustrates one of the by-ways of conservation. Hair plaster was required to repair/make good the heavily-haired daubed plaster in the Great Chamber and Inner Chamber (screen between the two rooms and window reveals on the north side). The hair used in the original, surviving heavily-haired plaster in particular, but also in other examples of haired plaster on the site, was ox-hair. Ox-hair was said to be unobtainable. It was reported that the modern tanning process made retrieval difficult, and also destroyed its strength and usefulness for plaster (pers comm Roger Scobie and Tony Leech). Besides, irrespective of this reported practical consideration, ox-hair was, apparently, barred from use in Britain on account of the danger of anthrax. The background to the anthrax scare is that there was an epidemic in Britain in the early years of this century, and many human deaths occurred as a result of virulent infection of animals, especially cattle. It has been suggested that there is therefore a possibility of anthrax infection in old plasters, and concern that the infection might be released again through the demolition and break-up of such old plasterwork. However, since the 1950s, figures of reported cases have dropped dramatically. The reported cases are mostly in the tanning, wool and leather industries: none has been reported in the construction industry. Statistics show that the high quantity of viable anthrax agents (eg bacteria) necessary to cause infection are extremely unlikely to be present in plaster. Instead of ox-hair, therefore, goat or yak-hair (a form of cattle, after all) were used extensively at Bowhill in the restoration. Horse-hair was regarded as too coarse and wiry and was not used. There are now several suppliers, but for 'ox' or 'cow', read 'yak' (information regarding anthrax from David Mason, English Heritage, and Alan Gardner, SPAB). Present day controls on imported animal hair are very strict.

45 See Blaylock (forthcoming). Traces of this later red and haired cob/lime plaster adhered over the original internal plaster which had been 'hacked' to accept it in many places.

46 The *locus classicus* for the use of lime water was Wells Cathedral. Partly in response, inconclusive clinical experiments were reported on by Price (1984) and Price & Ross (1984). See also Caroe & Caroe (1984) and Brereton (1991, 40 and fig 47). There are numerous conservators' reports which mention its use and it continues to be used, specifically recently in the consolidation of the plaster at Lacock Abbey, Wiltshire by the National Trust. Recently doubts about the efficacy of the method have been raised. See the comments by Richard Deane in the letters section of *SPAB News*, **18** (4), 1997.

47 In rough-casting the wall receives two coats of plaster or cement; and before the second coat is dry, a mixture of fine gravel and hot lime is thrown hard at it with a trowel, and sticks onto the second coat (Torr 1921, 48).

For 'hot lime' read lime in the process of slaking, a potentially hazardous procedure.

In the use of 'rough-cast' or 'slap dash', the Devon workmen are proficient. They render it pleasing to the eye and durable (Marshall 1796, **I**, 64).

The wall is first pricked up with a coat of lime and hair, on which when tolerably well set, a second coat is laid, as smooth as possible; as fast as the workman finishes this surface, another follows him with the rough-cast, with which he bespatters the fresh plastering, and smoothes it with a brush, so that the whole dries together. The rough-cast is a composition of small gravel, finely washed, mixed with pure lime and water to a state of semi-fluid consistency (Allen 1849–50, 40).

This last description appears to be derived from that of Loudon (1836). Alfred Howard differentiates clearly between 'rough-cast' which he describes as typically a 1:2:8 cement/lime/sand mix with coarse sand thrown on and 'scat' (also thrown on). SPAB advice (Townsend 1989) is for 1:3 lime-sand laying-on coats and 3:11 lime-sand casting coats, avoiding the use of cement. Note the relative 'weakness' of the finish coats, reducing the propensity to shrink.

48 Charles Smith stresses the importance of applying the render or plaster to the slurry coat at the appropriate moment. One area of lime-slurried internal stonework at Bowhill had to wait a month for its plaster coat because the slurry took that long to dry (works being carried out at an inappropriate time of year). 'Drying comes first, set later. The key is to have the water out so that compaction can follow' (pers comm Charles Smith). The operation is further complicated by the fact that differing backgrounds will cause different drying rates in the finish.

49 Unlike the usual builders' trowel, gauging trowels are not lozenge-shaped; they diminish gradually in width from their shoulders to a rounded tip. They are commonly used for plastering, especially finishing plaster in tight corners or to obtain special finishes (eg fresco). One was found on the wall-head of the Great Hall during repairs in the early 1980s. When the trial plaster panels were being undertaken on the underside of the 'roof-V' in the Great Hall, a gauging trowel was needed for use. At the time, the only one available on site happened to be the historic gauging trowel, kept in the Bowhill 'finds room'. Consequently for a short time it was once again pressed into service!

50 The specification was prepared by Richard Baker in consultation with Charles Smith.

51 It should be noted, however, that the 'one-coat' render solution may be a departure from recent mainstream practice, (seemingly extending back to the early nineteenth century and perhaps beyond) where two-coat work, ideally scat and finish coat, tends to be the preferred option. The Devon Earth Building Association (Bedford et al 1993) pamphlet on renders to stone and cob summarizes current good regional conservation practice and the modern technical view of the subject.

Glossary

Aggregate
Granular material, either processed from natural materials such as rock, gravel or sand, or manufactured such as slag (British Standards Institution 1984); the inert filler used in materials such as mortars, plasters, renders and concrete and naturally occurring or supplemented in earthen materials such as cob and daub.

Arris
'The sharp edge formed at the line where two planes meet' (Powys 1929 [1981], 200).

Ashlar piece
'Short vertical timber rising from the inner surface of a wall [or wall plate] to meet the common rafters' (Brunskill 1985, 92).

Batten
A long strip of timber of rectangular cross-section; a timber cover strip; the wide vertical boards of a framed, ledged and battened door. Commonly applied to horizontal sawn or riven strips of timber spanning the rafters of a roof to support the tiles or slates etc. These must be deep enough in cross-section to span between rafters without deflection when loaded, and wide enough not to split or deform when the coverings are suspended from or fixed to them.

Brace
'A subsidiary member in a timber frame located at an angle between two main timbers and stiffening them by [compression and] triangulation' (Brunskill 1985, 100). Wind-brace: a brace set in the plane of the roof and stiffening the rafters, purlins and trusses.

Carbonation
The chemical reaction of slaked lime (calcium hydroxide) with the carbon dioxide in the air, forming calcium carbonate. 'Carbonation should begin while the mortar is still drying out ... and will continue for many years' (Ashurst & Ashurst 1988b, 4).

Chase
A trench or groove cut in earth, timber or masonry building fabric to receive a pipe, electrical conduit, the edge of a metal flashing, etc.

Clay
1 'A natural, earthy, fine-grained material which develops plasticity when mixed with a limited amount of water; composed primarily of silica, alumina and water, often with iron, alkalis and alkaline earths' (Parker 1997, 58).
2 The fraction of a soil comprised of the smallest particles, that is finer than 2 microns.

May also refer to geological deposits in which clay is the predominant constituent, or, colloquially, to any fine-grained soil material which expands when wetted, becomes plastic and can be moulded when moist and shrinks and hardens on drying. It is in this last form that the term is generally used here.

Clay mineral
'One of a group of finely crystalline, hydrous silicates with a two- or three- layer crystal structure' (Parker 1997, 58).

Coarse stuff
A mixture of slaked lime putty and aggregate which is stored, protected from air, for as long as possible before being used as a base for lime mortar and render (Teutonico 1997, 43).

Collar
'A horizontal member in a roof spanning between a pair of inclined members, [usually principal rafters of a truss]' (Brunskill 1985 115).

Common rafter
'Rafters of equal scantling [cross-sectional area] found along the length of a roof, [sometimes supported off purlins between trusses]' (Coke *et al* 1982, 33).

Cornice plate
See Purlin.

Cruck
'Pairs of [long curved structural] timbers ... rising from, or near, ground level to meet at, or near, the apex of a roof [and forming the principal structure of certain types of roof construction]' (Brunskill 1985, 118).

Cruck-blade
'One of a pair of crucks' (Brunskill 1985, 118).

Cruck, jointed
A cruck-like truss in which the blades are made of two timbers jointed together, usually in the form of a curved-headed post supporting a principal rafter.

Day work joint
Site term denoting the limit of a day's work where this shows (usually as a line) in the completed fabric. In conventional West Country cob building the horizontal day work joint comes at the top of the course.

DEBA
Devon Earth Building Association, c/o Environment Directorate, Devon County Council, County Hall, Exeter EX2 4QW.

DEL
Directly Employed Labour

Dub-out
Preparing a wall or floor to take a smooth finish by filling uneven areas of the substrate with mortar or 'daub'.

EMAFU
Exeter Museums Archaeological Field Unit, now Exeter Archaeology

Fabric

The material components of a building or other man-made structure.

Feather edge

An edge (eg in mortar, earth plaster or timber) that is run out, or 'dies out', over adjacent surfaces.

Feather-out

The process of making a feather edge; for instance, to carry plaster over another surface, thinning it out until it 'dies out', rather than being 'checked' against a raised edge of that surface.

Fines

The fine particles in a mortar or earth mix.

Finish

A surface treatment applied to a substrate, eg plaster to walling, boards to floor structures.

Flash; Flashing

To make a weather-tight joint, or protect from penetration by rain, by lapping one surface over another; commonly a strip of impervious sheet material (often made of lead, zinc or copper) that excludes rainwater from the junction between a roof covering and another surface.

Flitch

In repair, a steel or iron plate inserted vertically and longitudinally into the centre of a timber beam and connected to it by bolts or by other means so that timber and metal perform as one composite structural unit; often used to stiffen or strengthen construction.

Flocculate

'To aggregate or clump together individual, tiny soil particles, especially fine clay, into small clumps or granules' (Brady 1974, 603).

Go-off

Term used with reference to the drying out or stiffening of mortar, plaster, cob, daub; To be no longer plastic, ie no longer readily workable but with strength not yet fully developed. Cob can still be pared, or shuttering stripped, at this stage.

Green

Plaster: Lime-based plaster adhering to the wall but still plastic enough to be worked with a trowel or beaten with a brush.
Timber: Timber containing sap which has not been seasoned or dried out and is therefore likely to warp if fixed beforehand.

Ground

A piece of timber fixed into, or onto, the face of a wall as a base for boards, plaster laths or window or door joinery.

Grout

'A thin [liquid] preparation of mortar which will flow into position [to fill voids]' (Jaggard & Drury 1949, 330).

Hanger

A timber or metal tensional support from which a component or structure is hung.

Hearting

Northern term for the core of a wall, usually composed of smaller material, or material different from its coursed, rubble or ashlar outside faces. It is sometimes formed of aggregates in a matrix of lime, cement or clay.

Humour

To bring new construction into line with the existing where it abuts in order to produce a visual softening of the junction. Essentially an aesthetic practice often arising from the fact that existing fabric has 'weathered' back from its original face line.

Initial set

'The first stage of hardening in concrete, mortar and plaster, before which all placing should be done' (McLean & Scott 1993, 241). In cob building, the term has been borrowed to refer to material that has 'gone off' (See Go-off).

Jack rafter

'Shortened common rafters running between eaves and hips or between ridge and valley' (Brunskill 1985, 170).

Jamb

'The side of an archway, doorway, window or other opening' (Coke *et al* 1982, 23).

Key

The roughness of a substrate surface, the texture of which enables plaster, mortar, coatings, etc. to grip with a mechanical bond; also to roughen or indent a surface.

Knock up

To re-mix concrete or mortar immediately before use, so as to improve its workability by creating enhanced plasticity. In cob building, the term is used colloquially to describe a similar process.

Laitance

A thin, opaque film of water and fine binder particles brought to the surface of a mortar or plaster by trowelling.

Lath

'A thin flat strip of wood, especially each of a series forming a ... support for plaster' (Oxford English Reference Dictionary 1995, 808). 'Lathing ... any groundwork intended to offer a key to plaster ... may be of sawn yellow deal (Baltic fir) or of oak, but the best laths are cleft .. These two kinds are known respectively as *sawn* and *ribben* laths' (Jaggard & Drury 1950, 284, 375).

Lay on, lay up

To spread on. With plaster, literally to 'lay it on with a trowel'. Also known in plastering as 'put up'.

Lime

General term for a binder used in mortars and plasters, which is derived from calcium or magnesium carbonate (limestone or dolomite) which has been burnt in a kiln and slaked. In this context, the term lime includes all of the oxides and hydroxides of calcium and magnesium, but excludes the carbonates (Holmes & Wingate 1997, 268). Colloquially, the term lime is also used to describe the ground limestone utilised by farmers to neutralise soil acidity and improve crop production.

Lime, hydrated

'Dry powder obtained by hydrating quicklime with enough water to combine chemically to form hydroxides. Hydrated limes may be high calcium limes (consisting mainly of calcium hydroxide) or *hydraulic limes* (q.v.). In the UK, the term hydrated lime is most commonly used to refer to a dry powder of non-hydraulic lime (calcium hydroxide)' (Teutonico 1997, 44). Hydrated lime powder is also known colloquially as 'bag lime'.

Lime, hydraulic

A form of lime which can set and harden under water. Natural hydraulic limes are produced by burning argillaceous (clayey) limestones and contain various amounts of calcium silicates and calcium aluminates in addition to calcium hydroxide. Several hydraulic limes of varying hydraulicity are presently available in dry hydrate form.

Lime putty, putty lime
'A form of slaked lime hydrate in a wet, plastic putty consistency, containing free water' (Teutonico 1997, 45). Lime putty is stored under water or in an airtight container before use to prevent the commencement of carbonation.

Lintel
'Horizontal beam of stone, timber, metal or concrete bridging an opening [to support overlying construction]' (Coke *et al* 1982, 24).

Make good
To replace, restore or complete that which has been damaged or is incomplete.

Make up
1   'To add extra material so as to bring something to the required level or quality' (McLean & Scott, 279).
2   To mix material or assemble components.

Mortar mill
A mechanised mixing machine consisting of a drum within which horizontally-mounted rollers turn around a central vertical rotating spindle. The height at which the rollers turn can be adjusted. Used to mix non-hydraulic lime mortar and also to make coarse stuff more plastic. Replaces the traditional practice of hand ramming and chopping lime mortars during preparation.

Needle
'A short timber, or wrought iron or steel beam, passed through a hole in a wall to give temporary support as in underpinning' (Brunskill 1985, 151).

Offset, set-off
The point at which the thickness of a wall diminishes, often found as a sloping ledge.

Packing
'Material used to fill up a space round or in something' (Oxford English Reference Dictionary 1995, 1044).

Piecing-in
See Tailing-in.

Pozzolan
A natural or manufactured material, containing reactive silica and alumina, which will combine with non-hydraulic lime in the presence of water to create a hydraulic set. Natural pozzolans of volcanic origin include pozzolana from Italy and trass from the Rhine region of Germany. Artificial pozzolans include PFA (pulverized fuel ash) and some brick dusts.

Principal
Heavy structural timber members forming the primary elements of an integrated trussed roof system.

Proud
'Slightly projecting from a surface' (Oxford English Reference Dictionary 1995, 1162).

Pulley groove
A shallow groove in a piece of material terminating in a socket or

mortice which allows another element to be slid into it at right angles.

Purlin
'A longitudinal member giving support to the common rafters of a roof and normally set at right angles to the slope of the rafters' (Brunskill 1985, 165). In the Bowhill context 'eaves purlin' is the purlin running at the level of the wall-head; also sometimes referred to here as 'cornice plate'.

Rack
The tendency of a frame or the trusses in a roof to lean sideways sometimes causing longitudinal collapse. Often occurs where there is lack of structural stability such as that given by diagonal bracing in the plane of the roof slope.

Requisition
Superintending Officer's (Specifier or Project Manager) Instruction to the contractor.

Resin
Widely (though somewhat inaccurately) used as a generic term to describe any synthetic polymeric compound used in conservation as an adhesive or consolidant.

Reveal
'Applied to all the exposed vertical surfaces [inside and outside] at the sides of an opening after the door or window frame has been fitted' (Jaggard & Drury 1949, 37–8).

Ring beam
Horizontal or cranked structural link of timber, steel, reinforced concrete etc, set on or within a wall and joining walls together continuously.

Riven lath
See Lath.

Scratch coat
First (render) coat of plaster in traditional two- or three-coat work. This is *scratched* to produce a key for adhesion of subsequent coats.

Scutch
To dress the surface of stone or cob using a scutch hammer.

Scutch hammer
Mason's tool for 'dragging' or 'combing' the surface of stone to produce a fine striated finish. Found to be useful at Bowhill for carefully paring back small cob repairs.

Shear key
A continuous projecting tile or timber tongue fixed vertically into one earth wall allowing a second adjacent wall to form a butt junction with the first without the need to form a physical bond between the two. Useful with cob where differential shrinkage is likely to occur where new is to be attached to existing walling.

Shear plane , slip plane
A plane of structural discontinuity within a wall.

Shelter coat
A protective, sacrificial coating for stone or plaster, usually composed of screened lime putty, fine aggregates and (sometimes) casein; intended to shield vulnerable historic material from both internal and external agents of decay.

Shillet
See endnote 23.

Slaking
The action of combining quicklime (calcium oxide) with water to produce calcium hydroxide (slaked lime in the form of lime putty or dry hydrate powder).

Slurry
'A semi-liquid mixture of fine particles and water' (Oxford English Reference Dictionary 1995, 1367).

Spike
A large nail, exceeding five inches in length.

Spike on
To fix in place by hammering-in spikes.

Splash coat
Colloquial; a wet coat of lime mortar or cement thrown or splashed onto a wall as a key for further finish coats.

Stopping
A filling for a hole; to fill a hole.

String
1   'An inclined board providing support for the steps and into which the treads and risers are housed and wedged' (Jaggard & Drury 1949, 228).
2   Shortened form of string course: a projecting ledge or straight visual line in construction. Usually a weathering detail, often used for horizontal visual emphasis.

Stud
'Lightweight timber members running vertically to help to divide a wall or partition into panels' (Brunskill 1985, 183).

Tailing-in
Fitting-in (or 'piecing-in') a wedge-shaped piece of masonry eg stone or brick into an irregular shape or gap.

Trestle pieces
Devon vernacular; timber end-bearing surface for a beam, transmitting its load to the supporting wall. These, in both timber and stone, have been known as 'templates' (see Jaggard & Drury 1949, 98). But see also Neve (1726 [1969], 255) 'Tassels, pieces of board that lie under the ends of the Mantletree'.

Valley board
'A wide board acting as the basis of a valley gutter at the internal angle of two meeting roofs' (Brunskill 1985, 185). The board is laid on top of the rafters, hence 'lay board'.

Weather, to weather
1   The process of degradation of a wall face or roof cladding due to the action of the weather over time.
2   To protect a vulnerable piece of material exposed to the action of the weather by means of a flashing, moulded overhang, etc.

Wichert
Local calcium carbonate and clay subsoil used for mud walling around a number of villages in Buckinghamshire ('white earth').

Wind-brace
See Brace.